SUTTON HARBOUR
CRISPIN GILL

To my wife Betty
who thought this the best of my
Plymouth books but who never
lived to see it published

SUTTON HARBOUR
CRISPIN GILL

DEVON BOOKS

First published in Great Britain in 1997

Copyright © 1997, Crispin Gill

*All rights reserved. No part of this publication may be
reproduced, stored in a retrieval system, or copied in any form
or by any means without the prior permission of the copyright holder.*

British Library Cataloguing in Publication Data

CIP record for this book is available from the British Library

ISBN 0 86114 912 2

DEVON BOOKS
Official Publisher to Devon County Council
Halsgrove House
Lower Moor Way
Tiverton
Devon EX16 6SS
Tel: 01884 243242
Fax: 01884 243325

The author and publisher acknowledge the generous support
provided by The Sutton Harbour Company towards the publication of this work.

Printed in Great Britain by BPC Wheatons Ltd

CONTENTS

Foreword		7
Acknowledgements		8
In the Begining		9
1.	Ownership	11
2.	Military Use	21
3.	Fishing	29
4.	Trade	39
5.	Quays and Railways	47
6.	Colonisation	58
7.	Houses, Churches and Pubs	66
8.	Work Ashore	81
9.	The Need for Change	93
10.	Bright New World	105
Index		118

SUTTON HARBOUR

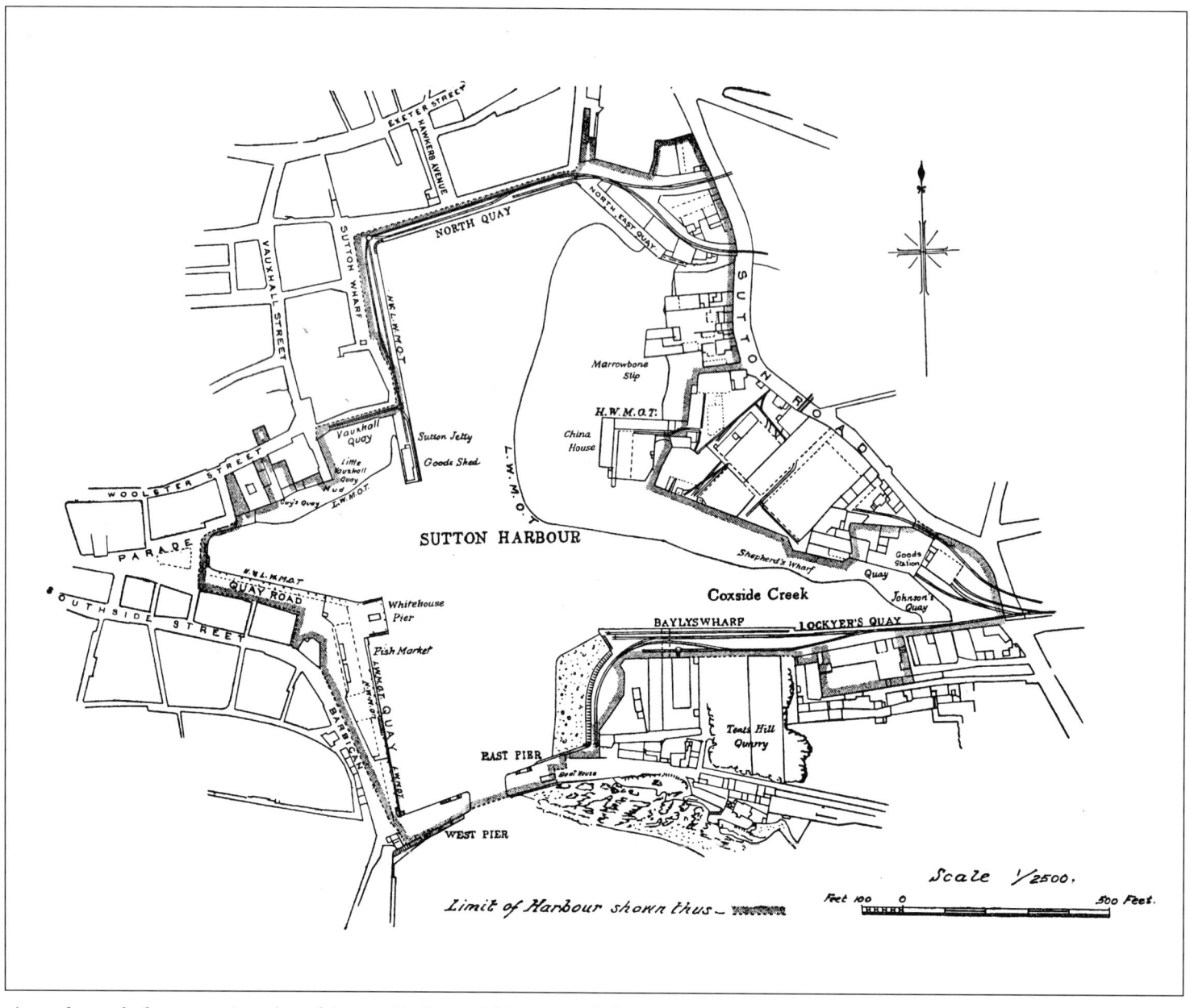

An early pre-lock, pre-marina plan of Sutton Harbour which names all the quays and is thus useful as a general guide and reference, for all such names appear throughout the book.

FOREWORD
by Duncan Godefroy

Duncan Godefroy

In the heart of old Plymouth lies the ancient port of Sutton Harbour. We do not know the name given to it by the little British community which had a few dwelling places on its shores, probably at Bretonside. When Saxon settlers came in from the sea they called it Suttone, the most southern 'town' in their Hundred of Walkhampton. The little town of fishermen grew up between the harbour and the early church of St Andrew, on the hill above the present harbour.

Over the centuries the harbour played a decisive role in national and world affairs, yet its shape remained virtually unchanged until the late eighteenth century, when the pierheads were built.

For nearly two hundred years the Sutton Harbour Company and its predecessors, the Sutton Harbour Improvement Company and the Sutton Pool Company, have had the responsibility of controlling and, for the last century, owning the harbour. Quays, roads and railways were constructed to provide facilities for its users.

But the decline in commercial shipping, and the changing needs of fishing, have led to enormous changes, including the award-winning extensive regeneration programme that has been carried out over the last five years.

In this third updated edition of his book, the renowned historian, Crispin Gill, chronicles the story of Sutton Harbour and its important history. It is a privilege to be a friend of the author but even more to be, with colleagues, the custodian of the harbour during the latter part of the twentieth century, in which time it has undergone so many exciting changes.

Duncan Godefroy JP
Managing Director
Sutton Harbour

ACKNOWLEDGMENTS TO THE 1976 EDITION

This study was written at the invitation of the Sutton Harbour Improvement Company, who gave me a free hand and in no way required me to write either as apologist or publicist. They generously opened their records to me, a privilege not previously given to any writer. The managing director, Mr Duncan Godefroy, gave me much help with the original and this revised edition, and another director, Mr Peter Stedman, made many useful suggestions in the revision. The archives of Devon County Record Office and the Duchy of Cornwall have also been examined; again not previously used for any study of the harbour. I am indebted to Sir Patrick Kingsley, the Secretary to the Duchy, and Mr S. A. Opie, the Record Clerk, for their help and courtesy. The former Plymouth City Librarian, Mr W. Best Harris, the late Mrs.Marion Beckford, local history librarian, and the late Mr J. Stevens, the archivist, also helped with their wealth of material. In the Plymouth archives of course one is constantly using the calendar of the records made by R. N. Worth, father of Hansford, so long chairman of Sutton Harbour.

I am grateful to the Western Morning News Co. Ltd and the City Library for permission to use their photographic files. The National Maritime Museum at Greenwich made remarkable restorations of some old photographs rescued from wartime damage. Thanks also to Andy Tucker.

I have concentrated my attention on the developments of the last two centuries because this is the least known period. The Elizabethan heroes have been sung many times; latter-day heroes like Francis Barnes of Holy Trinity are almost forgotten. My one regret is that so many stories have been left untold.

ACKNOWLEDGEMENTS TO THE 1997 EDITION

The last twenty years have probably seen greater changes in the harbour than at any time in its history. Which is my excuse for writing two up-dating chapters at such length. As ever I have had much help from Duncan Godefroy and Peter Stedman of the harbour company, and also from Patrick Marshall, the harbourmaster; Martin Emden, contracts manager; Peter Bromley, fishery manager; Shaun Lyth, Plymouth Trawler Agents; Chris Price, berthing master; and Zoe Thompson (who hunted down the difficult pictures).

Outside the harbour company I hope I have named in the text the people who run the multitudinous businesses by name; they have all found time to talk to me. Andrew Pye and Keith Ray brought me up-to-date on archaeological matters. Peter Edwards at the MAFF Fisheries Office helped with fishing statistics. But to all who have helped, and as ever to Betty my wife for her encouragement and support, my very real and heartfelt thanks.

I have one regret The first edition of this book started out as a minor summer job, and like Topsy just growed. As a result the first publication had to be squeezed into a pint pot in some haste; it never achieved an index let alone a list of sources and references. The index gap is filled with this edition but in no way, twenty years on, can I identify the sources of my information. Much came from the records of the Duchy of Cornwall, the City of Plymouth, the Custom House archives, and the Sutton Harbour Improvement Company. The histories of Worth and Jewitt were quarried. All I can really claim is that, as always, I used reliable sources.

IN THE BEGINNING

This book was originally written for publication by the Sutton Harbour Improvement Company in 1970. It was brought up-to-date and republished in 1976. By 1996, when the book was long out of print, it was decided to print another edition both to deal with the enormous changes that had happened to the harbour and its environs, and to mark the 150th anniversary of the founding of Sutton Harbour Improvement Company. But in spite of the concern of the harbour company with the book, it is a history of the whole harbour and its environs, not just the company.

It was also decided to put the third edition in the hands of an outside firm of publishers to make it available to a much wider circle of readers. The publishers were Devon Books, who had already reprinted the author's *Plymouth: A New History* and published a new work by him, *Plymouth River: The Cattewater and the Laira*. As this book is closely related to both the other two, it was agreed that the same format should be used as that of the other volumes, so that the three make a set, a matching trilogy. One day, perhaps, someone will do the same for Stonehouse and its Creek, Devonport and the Hamoaze. These are tasks for younger hands.

THE CHANGES

The past twenty years have seen enormous changes. Sutton Harbour has lock gates (and they were first proposed two centuries earlier, in 1786). The fish market for the first time in its history is now at Coxside, on the other side of the harbour. Commercial shipping has disappeared completely (the last ship, carrying coal, discharged its cargo in 1988). The fish market is booming, with some of the biggest trawlers in the United Kingdom fleet landing here and national merchants setting up their offices in the port. The marina is still the largest in Plymouth, and full. There are successful property developments all around the harbour.

Fishermen no longer live close around the harbour as they have done for centuries. Those that have not moved out to Southway find that the next-door flat is occupied by someone quite likely to have no connection at all with the area. A new middle-class element is moving in, living in blocks of flats carved from old warehouses or increasingly purpose-built. In the 1930s there were ten primary and elementary schools close around the harbour. Now there is only one.

Southside Street is no longer a village street with village shops. The antique shops which replaced them in the first of the postwar changes have all gone again from Southside Street, under the pressures of a yobbo culture which reached a peak in the late 1980s. (It must be noted that the harbour area, typical of all sea ports and fishing harbours, has always had a tough reputation. The difference now is that the disturbers of the peace come from other parts of the city, and are resented by the new inhabitants!). But some good quality restaurants have survived in the swarm of 'fast food outlets' and 'fun pubs'. Painters have hung on, art dealers of quality are back, gift shops

SUTTON HARBOUR

are improving in taste. Outside the high-summer weeks, when the ice-cream-licking trippers wander the streets like lost souls, the area is almost becoming two-faced, quiet pleasant people by day and the opposite by night. But even by night things are getting happier than they were.

Great efforts are being made to improve the area. Nowhere in the city is changing more rapidly, and for the better.

A panoramic view of Sutton Harbour today.

CHAPTER 1
OWNERSHIP

Sutton has been a royal port since there have been kings in England. When the Saxons reached the far west about the year 700 they gave away large tracts of land to encourage settlers, but Sutton was one of the few manors they kept in their possession. In due course the Norman kings gave it to the Valletorts of Trematon Castle, near Saltash, as a reward for faithful service. The family moved to a new house not far from the Sutton Pool and a little fishing village grew up under their wing, on the hill running up from the harbour to the mother church of St Andrew, patron saint of fishermen. With the march of time the Valletort line lost its vigour and in 1254 King Henry III granted a market in the little town to the Priors of Plympton, at a time when the monks had a good reputation as men of business.

But the port itself was still in the hands of the Crown. Within thirty years of the market grant a legal inquiry was held which laid down quite clearly that the port belonged to the King, and paid £4 a year to the Exchequer. The royal claim was through the feudal rights of Trematon, now vested in the King's brother, the Earl of Cornwall. When the last Earl died in 1310 and his estates reverted to the Crown, another lawsuit was needed to sort out the rival claims. The previous court hearing had held that the King held no land at Sutton; now the court ruled that six acres of land recovered from the sea beside Sutton Pool was royal property. Fishermen of the town used this land, sold their fish there and spread their nets to dry, paying the king a rent of twelve pence a year and a penny for each basket of fish. So the principle was established: land recovered from the sea was royal property, and the quays and warehouses built out across the bed of the harbour had to pay ground rent to the Crown or its successors in title.

When King Edward II gave the title of Earl of Cornwall to Piers Gaveston, the handsome young Gascon soldier who was so long his favourite, the earl held Sutton Pool because it was part of the 'water of Tamar' in the manor of Trematon. When the English barons killed Gaveston, his western holdings went to Edward's queen, Isabella, to whom the King granted a market in the port on two days a week.

The fishermen of Sutton knew nothing of these queer goings-on at court, but their next master was Edward the Black Prince. His father, King Edward III, made him the first Prince of Wales and Duke of Cornwall, and since his time the sovereign's eldest son has always held the Duchy from the hour of his birth. The Black Prince stormed in and out of Sutton Pool like his great-grandfather, Edward I, always busy with his French wars. But what really mattered to the Sutton fishermen was not so much their royal landlord, but the men who 'farmed' or rented the harbour from the Duchy, and the efficiency of their bailiffs or stewards.

A fisherman mending nets on West Pier in the days of sail and steam trawlers. The right to spread nets on the quays, and on the Hoe, goes back to a court ruling of 1310.

SUTTON HARBOUR

An early lessee of Sutton Harbour, John Sparke, lived at the Friary. This gateway to the property survived in Exeter Street into the nineteenth century, opposite the Sutton Road turning.

Captain McBride, who as a Plymouth MP was instrumental in having the piers at the entrance to Sutton Harbour built in 1790-9, gave his name to this pub and his portrait appears on the sign.

Sometimes the lessees were powerful local businessmen, like John Sparke in 1617 who lived in the Friary (between Beaumont House and the junction of Exeter Street and Sutton Road) and could look across the Pool from his windows. He shared the lease with John Fowell, another Plymouth businessman.

In 1628 the lease went to a group of knights, all unknown locally, but they assigned it through various people until in 1640 it was held by the 'governors, assistants, wardens and poor people of the Hospital of Orphan's Aid', the charity which the Puritan merchants of the town had built in 1616. After the Civil War the possessions of the Duchy were 'settled on trustees for the use of the Commonwealth'. In fact Plymouth Corporation was in effective control for twenty years or more, and as in 1637 they had bought the manor of Sutton Valletort from the Hawkins family (they already held the manor of Sutton Prior), they claimed that the land between low water mark and high water mark belonged to them and not the Duchy. It was to be a sore point between the two authorities for the next two centuries.

LAW SUITS

After the Restoration, King Charles II moved sharply against the town which had fought so hard against his father. He refused the Corporation a new lease, because of their former depredations, and his new tenant was Colonel Richard Arundel, one of the staunchest Royalists in Cornwall right through the Civil War and the Commonwealth. The King made him a peer and Lord Arundell went to court, obtaining by 1664 a decree that the Duchy ownership of Sutton Pool extended to the high water mark. The Corporation lost an income of £100 a year and suffered heavy legal costs, and a number of citizens who had built houses and cellars on the harbour bed found themselves Duchy tenants. This success persuaded Lord Arundell to sue the Corporation next for the two existing quays, but he seems to have lost this. In 1684 Plymouth asked him for a sub-lease of the harbour but his terms were too high, and in 1691 a sub-lease went to Edward Tregenna and Peter Courtenay.

From 1720, when the future George II was Prince of Wales the Pool was 'in hand', that is the Duchy managed it directly, and the detailed records of the period are still in the Duchy of Cornwall archives at Buckingham Gate. But the sub-tenants refused to acknowledge the Duchy as their landlords, and even took leases from the Corporation. Eventually the Duchy solved this unsatisfactory position by finding a new tenant who was near at hand and could cope with the sub-tenants. He was Robert Hewer who had inherited in 1737 the pleasant house at Manadon which was, until 1995 when the college closed, the official residence of the captain of the Royal Naval Engineering College. He took the lease of Sutton Harbour in 1743 and though he died within a few years the lease passed to the Hall family, his heirs. During the Hewer-Hall regime, which was marked by incessant law-suits against sub-tenants for the first ten years, the Duchy did very well for, apart from an annual rent of £13 8s 6d, they also collected at least three 'fines' of £1000 when leases were renewed. Thomas Veale, a lessee during this period, battled with the Corporation over boundaries and in 1753 the sheriff's officers even seized the town mace because Plymouth had not entered a reply to a charge against them. Humphrey Hall, last male heir, died in 1801 and left the estate to three daughters who wrangled in the courts until Mrs Hall-Parlby won Manadon. Her family remained there until the early years of this century.

The first ten years of the nineteenth century could not have been a worse time for Sutton Harbour to endure uncertain ownership. It had already been dragged into politics. For most of the eighteenth century Plymouth had been a 'pocket' borough where the two or three hundred electors regularly returned the candidates put up, first both by the Admiralty and towards the end of the century by the Admiralty and the Prince of Wales. By 1780 the freeholders of Plymouth were fighting this system and in 1784 managed to elect a serving naval officer, Captain John McBride, 'an exceedingly troublesome, busy, violent man', who defeated the Government's nominee. He is greatly credited with obtaining the Government grants which built the piers across the entrance to Sutton Harbour in 1791 and 1799, but he was actually out of Parliament in 1790 and back at sea as an admiral.

But the piers were a mixed blessing because, by cutting down the scour of the tides, they caused the harbour to silt up. It was so bad that by 1806 the Pool was drying out on every spring tide, right to the inlet between the piers. As a growing population was also sending more sewage into the Pool the whole town was made acutely aware that something had to be done.

The first need was to resolve the ownership of the lease. There seems to have been two rivals who were anxious to take over from the disputing Hall heirs: Colonel John Hawker the wine merchant and William Elford the banker. Plymouth Corporation was also trying to get the lease into municipal hands. But the Duchy were suspicious. 'Plymouth Corporation would like to seize the Duchy land because they hold the manor of Sutton Prior... they have been trying to get hold of Sutton Harbour ever since their lawsuit with the present lessee in 1754', wrote Robert Gray, secretary of the Duchy, in various 1805 letters. Nor were they any happier with the merchants in business around the Pool, who were constantly building out into Duchy land. The Duchy also had a new champion in the field.

IMPROVERS

Thomas Tyrwhitt had just started to build Dartmoor Prison to relieve the congestion in the prisoner-of-war barracks at Millbay. A friend and protege of the Prince of Wales since university days, he had already leased 2300 acres of Dartmoor and built Tor Royal as his home there; now he was creating a new village which he called Prince Town. He had just been appointed Lord Warden of the Stannaries, the Duchy's highest office, and in his improving zeal he was looking round for fresh fields. 'I had hit upon a plan by which the lease of Sutton Pool may be delivered over to the Prince (of Wales) which will make Plymouth ever after lay at His Royal Highness's feet', he wrote in October 1805. In 1806 when Philip Langmead, a local man who had won a place as Member of Parliament against the Crown nominees, resigned in disgust, Tyrwhitt moved into his seat. The businessmen were not pleased to have yet another Crown member, who was a Duchy officer into the bargain.

Now Tyrwhitt upset them still more with a plan to improve Sutton Harbour. Basically it was an adaptation of one put forward in 1786 by William Simpson, a Duchy surveyor, to make a wet dock at the top of the harbour. Dock gates would be opened at high tide to allow ships to enter and leave, then they would be closed and the ships inside would always remain afloat alongside the quays, and safe from any weather.

A meeting of 'merchants, shipowners, traders and inhabitants' was called in the Guildhall in

SUTTON HARBOUR

February 1806 to debate the plan; and it was resolved to oppose it because it would entail heavy tolls without adequate advantages. Three men were appointed to talk to Thomas Lane, Humphrey Hall's old partner who was the surviving lessee.

Lane was found to be willing to assign the lease for £20 000 and was offered £15 000. By April the Duchy had a report on the state of the Pool. Daniel Alexander, their surveyor, disliked the dock and was gloomy about the trade prospects of the harbour but, more important, the Admiralty was objecting to any wet dock. So by 1807 Tyrwhitt's plan was shelved and forgotten, and Lane was only asking £10 000 for the lease—and only getting offers of £8000.

The Tyrwhitt plan was dead, but there was a new 'improver' in the field. In December 1806 the vigorous Lord Boringdon at Saltram, who became the first Earl of Morley in 1815, gave notice that he proposed laying a trot of moorings in the Cattewater. He had been building up his property at Turnchapel since 1798, and had established two shipyards which were already building large warships. Now commercial ships would be able to pick up his moorings, and barges land their cargoes at Turnchapel. The Admiralty quibbled, the Crown fretted, there was another meeting in Plymouth Guildhall (though poorly attended), and a letter to the Duchy saying that the mooring chains in the Cattewater would take trade from Sutton Harbour. But Lord Boringdon got his mooring chains, and Sutton did not really suffer. When the Admiralty later made Lord Boringdon pick up his moorings to be re-sited, there were appeals from forty-eight captains and shipbuilders, the Plymouth pilots and eight Plymouth merchants, for them to be relaid. It was really only a development of the ancient principle, that the Cattewater was the deep-water anchorage and Sutton Pool the dock through which the goods passed.

LOCALS TAKE OVER

Three memorials went up to the Prince's Council in 1809; the first two from ship owners and masters complaining that their vessels were being damaged by grounding on anchors and stones; and the third saying that a group of local men were anxious to build a dock within the Pool. But nothing happened and by November 1809 Richard Bayly, the timber merchant, was refusing to pay any dues because of the state of the harbour. The Corporation and the merchants closed their ranks, the Duchy overcame its suspicions, and after a series of meetings in Plymouth Guildhall and with the Plymouth lawyer Henry Woollcombe constantly in London negotiating, the whole position was changed. In 1810 John Hawker took over the lease of Sutton Pool on a fine of £13 000, on 26 June 1811 the royal assent was given to the Sutton Pool Act, and in 1812 the Prince Regent gave to the Sutton Pool Company formed under the Act a 99-year lease—for a fine of £6000.

The proprietors of the new company had to meet in the King's Arms in Bretonside on the Monday fortnight after the passing of the Act to put it into execution. Many familiar names were among their ranks: Balkwill the chemist, Bayly, Hawker and Collier the wine merchants, Cookworthy (whose father had discovered china clay and made the first porcelain in England), Derry (whose son built Derry's Clock), Elford the banker, Lockyer (remembered in Lockyer Street), Moore the shipbuilder, Luscombe the ship-owner, Prance, Pridham, Rodd, Sir Michael Seymour (remembered in Seymour Road), George Soltau. They had authority to raise £50 000 for building

14

quays, wet and dry docks, storehouses, and so forth.

The company spent much money on improving the harbour and, in spite of the inflated wartime returns from shipping, did not show a surplus until its sixth year. For the first time the businessmen of Plymouth had control of their own harbour, could run it to suit their own affairs, and improve it as they saw fit. All should have been well, and was for some years. But the birth of the Sutton Pool Company almost matched in time the birth of the age of steam, which was to bring bigger changes in sea and land transport than had ever been seen before.

STEAMSHIP

Plymouth saw its first steamer, the paddler *Duke of Argyle*, on passage from the Clyde to London, as early as 1815. The first one built in the port, the *Sir Francis Drake*, was launched from Brown's Yard at Cattedown in 1823, and steamers on regular service between Ireland and London were calling by 1825. In November 1834, when the extension of the Great Western Railway from Bristol to Exeter seemed assured, a crowded meeting in Plymouth Guildhall welcomed the idea of extending the line to Plymouth and at the close £20 000 was subscribed. Steam on land and sea were closely linked; the great Isambard Kingdom Brunel was promising the Bristol merchants a western terminus not in their port but in America and he was building the massive *Great Western* steamship to make that possible. By 1836 Brunel was also surveying a possible railway route from Exeter to Plymouth, but the early enthusiasm in the port had waned and nothing came of it.

The *Great Western* made her first crossing from Bristol to New York in April 1838, to inaugurate the first regular Atlantic ferry service. A rival company sent the smaller *Sirius* across to beat the *Great Western* into New York by a few hours, and on 16 July 1838 the *Sirius* anchored in the Cattewater to land the American mail, about 3000 letters and newspapers, at the Barbican steps.

A new man had arisen in Plymouth during these years, Thomas Gill. He was the first Mayor of the town, in 1835, under the Municipal Reform Act. This had followed the Parliamentary Reform Act of 1832, which Plymouth heartily welcomed as finally freeing it from Crown nominees as members of Parliament.

Thomas Gill, who was also Member of Parliament for Plymouth in 1841-6, had made enough money to rent Buckland Abbey as his home. He had some property in Sutton Harbour but his main interest was the huge limestone quarry which was steadily removing West Hoe, and the limekilns there. The floor of the quarry stretched from the cliff edge to the shores of Millbay but in the bay north of this there was only one cottage, beside a sandy cove, where Mrs. Kingdom hired out bathing machines. A soap factory and a brown-paper mill occupied the site of the old manorial tidal mills at the head of the bay, the clubhouse of the Royal Western Yacht Club stood at the corner of Hobart Street and Buckingham Place looking across a few yachts at anchor, and the Royal Marine Barracks was on the very edge of the western shore. Otherwise Millbay was in its natural state.

MILLBAY CHALLENGE

Within fifteen months of *Sirius* landing the American mail in the Cattewater, Gill announced plans to build Millbay Pier. Six months later Plymouth was visited by commissioners examining the rival merits of the Channel ports as pack-

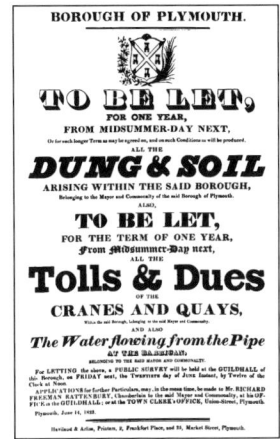

The Borough of Plymouth had its own property and rights around the harbour. This 1823 notice, among other things, offers to rent the right to remove the street sweepings (largely horse manure) from the quay where they were dumped; they were taken by barge up the Tamar to fertilise the market gardens there.

SUTTON HARBOUR

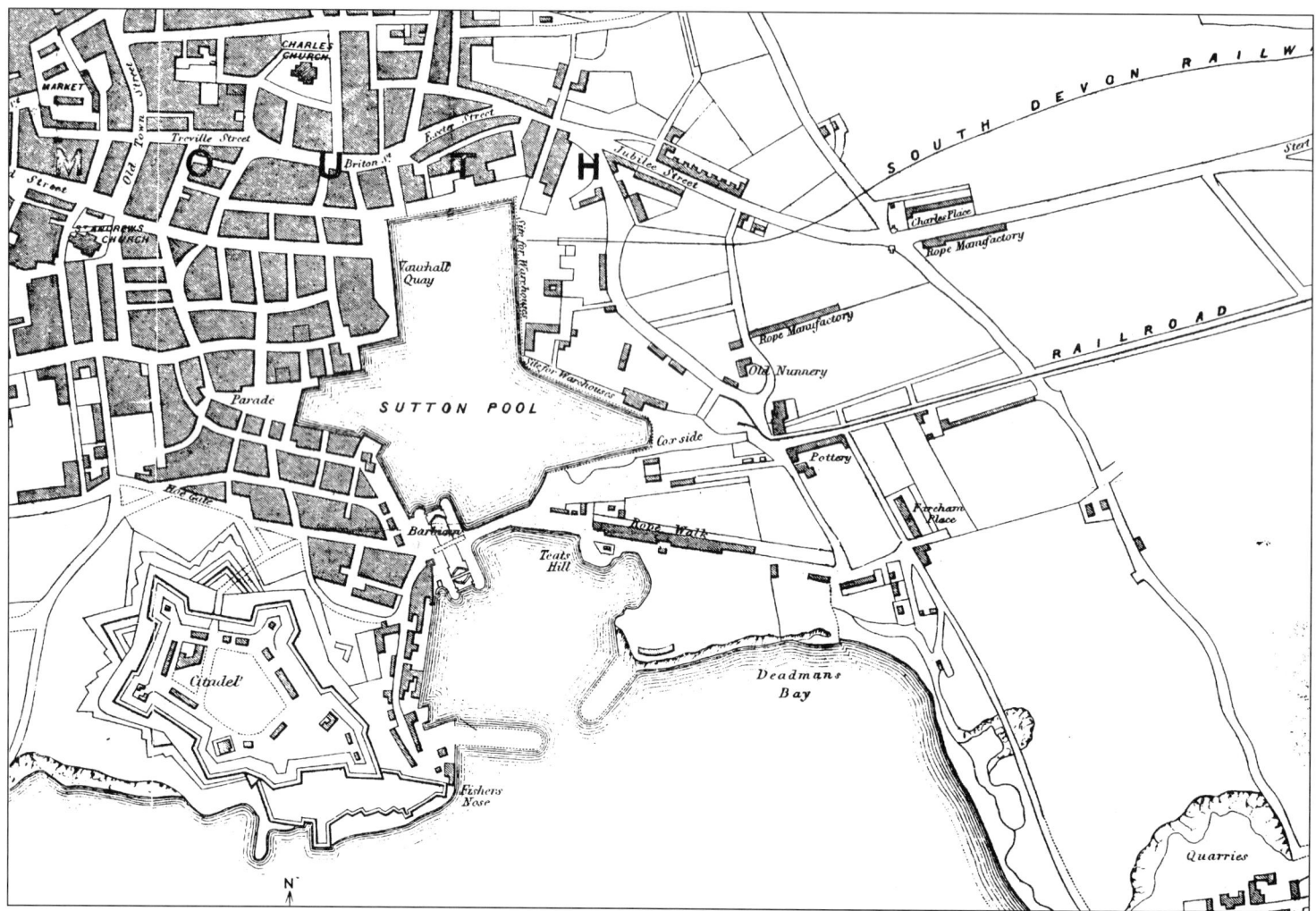

Brunel's 1845 plan to put lock gates at the entrance to Sutton Harbour; it would be 150 years before it was finally achieved.

et stations, and the burden of the Plymouth evidence was the town's advantages for the West Indian and Mediterranean mails. Gill had his pier open by 1844, after spending £27 000. It could berth 3000-ton ships alongside, and was 500ft long.

Here was a serious challenge to Sutton Harbour for the port's trade, especially as on 4 July 1844 the South Devon Railway Act received the royal assent. This approved the building of a railway line from Exeter to Plymouth, to which the Great Western Railway was the main subscriber, with a terminus planned near Eldad and a branch line to Millbay. What is more, the South Devon Railway Company's chairman was Thomas Gill. Millbay Pier and the new railway seemed firmly linked together. There was a gleam of hope for Sutton Harbour, however. The

Act would not permit locomotives on the Millbay branch. It had to cross Stonehouse Lane (King Street), Union Street, and Millbay Road on level crossings, which meant a gradient in one place of 1-in-25. The first annual general meeting of the railway company at the Royal Hotel, Plymouth, decided to move the terminus from Eldad to Union Street, to get a branch line from Laira to Sutton, and to alter the Millbay branch. New Parliamentary powers were obtained which granted all these changes, but the Millbay branch still had to cross Union Street on the level and locomotives were still forbidden. The railway would reach Sutton Harbour but not Millbay.

In November 1844 advertisements appeared in the *Plymouth, Devonport and Stonehouse Herald* for the Sutton Harbour and Dock Company. Arrangements had been completed for the transfer of the property of the Sutton Pool Company to the new body, to turn Sutton Harbour into a floating dock, and to link up with the main line railway. Obviously the new company was formed to raise the extra capital that would be needed. It was not a take-over, the solicitors were still Woollcombe and his partners, as for the 1811 company, and many of the old names appear on the provisional committee. There were also new ones : the company was composed of the mercantile strength of Plymouth. Among members were the Earl of Morley (president of the Chamber of Commerce), Alger, Bayly, the two Bryants: Bulteel, Prance and Derry the bankers, Irving Clarke of Efford Manor and Col. Elliott of the Barley House, Fox, Hawker, Luscombe, P. E. Lyne the Mayor, Sir George Macrath the naval surgeon (an old friend of Nelson), Moore, Robert Scott of Outlands (who had a brewery in Hoegate Street and whose grandson was Robert Falcon Scott of the Antarctic), Henry Woollcombe, and Dr James Yonge. The engineer was I. K. Brunel himself, and his plans for the improvement of Sutton Harbour were deposited with the Clerk of the Peace at Plymouth before November 30 that year, just as a vast collection of plans for new railways were rushed to the Clerk of the Peace in the Castle at Exeter, so that they could be presented to Parliament in the following year.

RAILWAYS JOIN IN

It was a great jostling for position - the railway 'scrimmage' one local paper called it - at the start of a race whose prizes were enormous. Because ships had difficulty in carrying enough coal for the Atlantic crossing a western port was vital, and there was also no established packet port in the Channel. Southampton had only just started building modern docks, which already had more business than they could accommodate. It could still be challenged. The railway behind Southampton's rebirth, the London & Southampton, later the London & South-Western, was trying to get a south coast route to the Westcountry to fight the GWR. In turn the GWR could fight back by making Plymouth a port to rival Southampton. A ship calling at Plymouth would get its passengers and mail to London by train far more quickly that if it steamed on to Southampton to disembark them there. The prize at stake was the steamship passenger and mail traffic of the Americas and Africa, India, the Orient and Australia. With Millbay only linked to the main line by horse-drawn trains and steep gradients, the GWR was investing in Sutton Harbour, which it could reach. That was why the new wet dock for Sutton Harbour was designed by Brunel, the GWR engineer. The Duchy was backing the Sutton Harbour plan, and opposing the railway extension to Millbay. The Sutton Pool Company was prosperous, with a revenue averaging £2500 for the previous three years, and its rent to the Duchy only £759 a year.

But Sutton Harbour's dreams were short-lived. The Admiralty were once again the villains. In July 1846 they refused to permit Sutton Pool being made into a floating dock, because without lock gates it served as a harbour of refuge. But there were no such objections to Millbay being made into a dock - the Plymouth Great Western Dock Company had deposited its plans at the same time as the Sutton Harbour and Dock Company. The main line reached Laira in May 1848 and a year later was across Union Street on a bridge, to a terminus at Millbay. The Great Western Docks were being built, with the South Devon Railway contributing £15 000, the Bristol & Exeter Railway £7500 and the GWR another £7500. Early in 1850 the GWR main line was linked to Millbay Docks and in December of that year, when special ceremonies marked the inauguration of Plymouth as a Government mail-packet station, the steamer *Bosphorus* was loaded with the Cape mails in Millbay. The GWR line to Sutton Pool was completed in 1852, but the traffic was already going to Millbay.

IMPROVEMENT COMPANY

The Sutton Harbour and Dock Company was dead before it was founded. Its leading promoters were now directors of the South Devon Railway and its allied dock company, with Thomas Woollcombe chairman of the railway after Gill, original developer of Millbay, had resigned from the chair of the South Devon. So another company was launched to take over Sutton Harbour. It was authorised under an Act of Parliament in 1847, as the Sutton Harbour Improvement Company, but it was a smaller venture than had been originally planned. The old shareholders were bought out for £2400 and 584 of the new £25 shares. Only two names survived from the 1811 list of directors, Luscombe the shipowner and broker, and Soltau. The new directors included John Alger and William Burnell, with soap and chemical factories at Coxside; Thomas Pethick the merchant and contractor, John Pope the sail and rope-maker of Teat's Hill, and two appointed by the London & South-Western Railway Company.

Abandoned by one railway company, Sutton Pool had turned to another. That year L&SWR had promoted in Parliament the Cornwall & Devon Central & Plymouth Railway, intending to reach Plymouth north of Dartmoor and down through Tavistock. They were willing to advance capital to Sutton Harbour to secure accommodation for their traffic there. The new Act gave the Improvement Company not only powers to improve the harbour but also to build railway lines. But the L&SWR was no nearer than Southampton in 1847, and it was not to reach Plymouth until 1876.

The final arrival of the L&SWR produced the biggest of all changes in the ownership of Sutton Pool. In the same year, 1876, the Improvement Company secured a new Act of Parliament which gave them the right to purchase the harbour from the Duchy for £38 000. How far their hopes of rapid development were fulfilled is indicated by the fact that they still had not completed the purchase within the ten years scheduled in the Act. Their option was extended to Lady Day 1892, and the actual completion was on 17 March 1891. They were a long time, fifteen years, about the business. What they bought was 'all the water, soil and pool of Sutton situate near the Borough of Plymouth' with all the ancient rights of the Duchy to levy charges on ships entering harbour, every piece of cargo loaded or unloaded, and a

OWNERSHIP

charge on fishing boats coming in, plus the dues laid down in various Acts for use of the quays.

Apart from the tidal area, the company also acquired a certain amount of property which had been built out over the original harbour bed (though not all, by a long way). An agreement had been reached in 1757 with the Corporation, after the long squabbles, as to which land was Duchy and which was Corporation owned, and this is still the basis on which ownership is divided. It did not end the arguments with the Corporation. The town opposed the very first 1811 Bill on the grounds that it would levy heavy rates without corresponding advantage. There was always the fear in the mind of the Corporation that the public interest in the harbour would be sacrificed to provide profit.

The directorate of the company shows a subtle change over the years, reflecting the change in harbour use. Up to the inter-war period all the chairmen were in businesses largely concerned with the maritime life of the port: William Fox and his successor William Luscombe (1864-84) were shipping agents, Thomas Pitts (1884-90) a maltster, Robert Bayly (1891-1901) a timber merchant, Andrew Saunders Harris (1901-8), Sir Joseph Bellamy (1908-18) a shipping agent, H. J. Longford (1918-23).

From 1923 to 1950 Hansford Worth, the great Dartmoor scholar, was chairman, but he was by profession a civil engineer and for over fifty years was the company's engineer as well. W. J. W. Modley (1950-60) was managing director of Bigwoods ice works and he was succeeded by Charles W. Turner (1960-4), a solicitor. The next chairman, C. J. Woodrow (1964), was another engineer who was engineer to the company before becoming chairman, but he was also managing director of Blight & White, originally a Stonehouse engineering firm, one of the major steel construction companies in the south of England.

In the bleak days of the First World War the company sold off some of its property round the harbour, such as the warehouse (since rebuilt) of Plymouth Co-operative Society on North Quay in 1916, and the yard of Plymouth Coal Co. Ltd. In the time of Charles Turner the company realized the value of its land holdings round the harbour and started developing with new buildings and leases.

One effect of this expansion time, for the company was buying land rather than selling, was to enhance considerably the value of its shares on the Stock Market. With the steady improvement of commercial shipping after the Second World War the company was in good health: when that began to falter after 1969 the new developments in fishing and yachting enabled the company to spend more money on the harbour and show

The Barbican before the old fish market was built in 1890. This was still on the line of the Hawkins quay of 1572. Luscombe and Bellamy, partners in the ship-broking business seen on the right, were both chairmen of the Sutton Harbour Improvement Company.

SUTTON HARBOUR

The Sutton Harbour Company's office on Guy's Quay. The warehouse behind, like so many others, is now an antiques centre.

good dividends. The £25 shares which stood at £9-9s in 1850 were at £52-53 in 1959. They were subsequently sub-divided into 25p units and in 1976 were quoted at 73-75p.

But the harbour by 1976 was no longer the city's primary source of wealth and its directors were all professional men not, like their predecessors, drawing their livelihood from its activities. The Right Hon. Baroness Hornsby-Smith, DBE, was the only non-resident director apart from the railway men. The deputy chairman was Mr P. C. Stedman, a chartered surveyor, and the managing director and secretary was Mr Duncan Godefroy.

The other directors were Mr J. M. Luscombe (no relation to the old shipping family), a stockbroker, and Mr R. G. W. Pengelly, a chartered accountant. Messrs. J. L. Sampson and B. R. J. Yandell were appointed by the British Railways to the Board, and the Ministry of Defence representative was the Assistant Queen's Harbour Master. He represented the fact that, to some extent, Sutton Pool was still a royal port. It is a 'creek' within the limits of a Royal Dockyard, as defined by an Act of 1865, and as such is still within the jurisdiction of the Queen's Harbour Master of Plymouth.

CHAPTER 2
MILITARY USE

Wine, fish and war, in that order, were the three trades that made Sutton Harbour and, through the harbour, Plymouth. King Edward I first chose the port as a base for his French wars in 1297, and it kept that role for nearly 200 years, until the end of the Hundred Years War. In that time Sutton Harbour was the base from which seven major expeditions sailed for either France or Portugal, and the main port handling all the business of maintaining a force overseas. The great men of the day became familiar figures on the quayside. King Edward I was here for a month, with his brother Edward Crouchback, Earl of Lancaster. His great-grandson, the Black Prince, was best known; he took out the biggest fighting force of all to win the battle of Poitiers and came back into the harbour with King John of France as his prisoner. His sister the Princess Joan and his son, Richard of Bordeaux, later King Richard II, used the port; his brother, John of Gaunt, was in residence at the Whitefriars for a time.

All this brought much business to the port, for soldiers have to be fed and ships repaired. What problems came in the train of the odd thousand men, some the scum of the gaols of England, left idle about the port for a whole summer, are another matter. It also brought attention from the enemy; almost the first French move in the Hundred Years War was to burn the English Channel ports, Plymouth amongst them. That 1337 raid may have been the worst, for big ships in Sutton Harbour were burnt, part of the town, and eighty-nine Plymouth men killed.

Thenceforward the town defences improved; and though there were another half a dozen raids, the French never got into Sutton Harbour again or into Plymouth proper. In the last raid of 1403 they did get up the Cattewater and attack Plymouth from behind, but it is likely that they only burnt the Bretonside houses, outside the town walls.

At the foot of Lambhay Hill, behind the Admiral McBride pub, a round tower of random limestone is all that remains of the four-castled fort built in these years to guard Sutton Pool. By itself it could not have kept a ship out of the harbour, but a chain stretched across the narrow mouth did, and the fort with its primitive guns and its bows and arrows stopped boats coming in to cut the chain, or lower it. In spite of the damage that the French did in that century of war, the fort preserved the harbour and crippled the French attacks on the town. Its four towers are still on the Plymouth coat of arms, arranged around the St Andrew's cross of the mother church. Its watergate, or barbican, stood at what is now the base of the Western Pier.

The French wars fizzled out in the anarchy of the Wars of the Roses. Piracy, always rife in the Channel when English authority was weak, did not die out when the more vigorous Yorkist

SUTTON HARBOUR

Archaeologists are increasingly challenging the idea that this curved structure is all that remains of the four-towered medieval castle that guarded the entrance to Sutton Harbour. But it is on the site. The piers at the harbour entrance did not exist in those days and the castle guarded a chain across the harbour to prevent enemy ships from entering. The little garden in front was created by Lady Astor for the enjoyment of retired fishermen and local pensioners. This 1968 photograph shows the coal wharf still in use.

Edward IV won the throne. When Plymouth complained to him in 1460 that corsairs had raided the town, burnt much of it, taken prisoners, and even stolen jewels from the church, he calmly authorised the town to sue the Pope for a Bull of Excommunication against all further offenders. All the evidence, as Edward IV was no doubt aware, points to this having been an attempt to land French support for the Lancastrian cause. In 1470 when Warwick the Kingmaker came ashore in Sutton Pool with the King's turncoat brother, the Duke of Clarence, they were dined by Mayor Yogge and the imprisoned Lancastrian Henry VI was proclaimed King in Plymouth Guildhall. The short results were that Yogge was put out of office; Warwick killed in battle; and Clarence, in due course, drowned in the butt of Malmsey.

WAR WITH SPAIN

A new quay was built in 1572, now called the Barbican, to accommodate the privateers, English, French and Dutch, who made up a Protestant fleet raiding the Spanish ships taking arms and money to their armies in the Low Countries. Hawkins of Plymouth was admiral of this motley company: Dutch sea-beggars, French Huguenots, English ships financed by half the gentry of Devon, fighting the war against Catholic Spain which cautious Elizabeth could not bring herself to declare. When this struggle, half religious, half for control of the seas, spread into the Spanish colonies across the Atlantic it was Plymouth men and Plymouth ships which still led the way. A cousin of the Hawkins family, Francis Drake, got behind the Spanish by passing Cape Horn and raiding their unguarded Pacific coast. He had to get home by sailing round the world, the first Englishman (and only the second ship) to do so. He started and finished his voyage in Sutton Harbour in a ship only twice as long as Francis Chichester's *Gipsy Moth*, and he sailed the hard route against wind and current all the way. Drake went on to whip the Spanish in West Indian waters, in their home ports, and finally in the Channel when they brought up their great Armada. Sutton Harbour was always his base and, with the Plymouth men who commanded and crewed his ships, he gave England a supremacy at sea that lasted for three-and-a-half centuries, made England a world power and ensured that North America was developed by the Anglo-Saxon Protestants and not, like South America, by the Roman Catholics of the latin countries. In the forty years after 1560 the shape of the modern world was decided by the ships and men from Sutton Pool.

Francis Drake, the three generations of Hawkinses, Oxenham, Ralegh, Grenville, Frobisher, Gilbert, Davis, all the great Elizabethan seamen worked out of Plymouth. Thomas Candish (or Cavendish) started and finished the third circumnavigation of the world in Sutton Pool, setting out on Drake's route in 1586 and meeting the scattered ships of the defeated Armada as he struggled home across the Bay of Biscay.

Drake left Plymouth two legacies, apart from fame. One was the water supply which he brought in from Dartmoor (it watered not only the houses but the ships as well); the other was a fort to replace the old one, which only guarded the Pool. Henry VIII had built a tower at Fisher's Nose to guard the Cattewater and the town had extended this with a series of gun platforms. Their walls now hold up the pavement between Fisher's Nose and the Royal Plymouth Corinthian Yacht Club. Drake's fort on top of the Hoe completed the effectiveness of these defences. Ironically its only war was against the King of England.

This model of Plymouth as it looked in 1620 was exhibited in the Mayflower *celebrations of 1970. A conjectural medieval fort can be seen above the houses on the Barbican, with Drake's 1590s fort on the Hoe in the background.*

Sir John Hawkins, admiral of the privateering fleet for which the original Barbican quay was built.

SUTTON HARBOUR

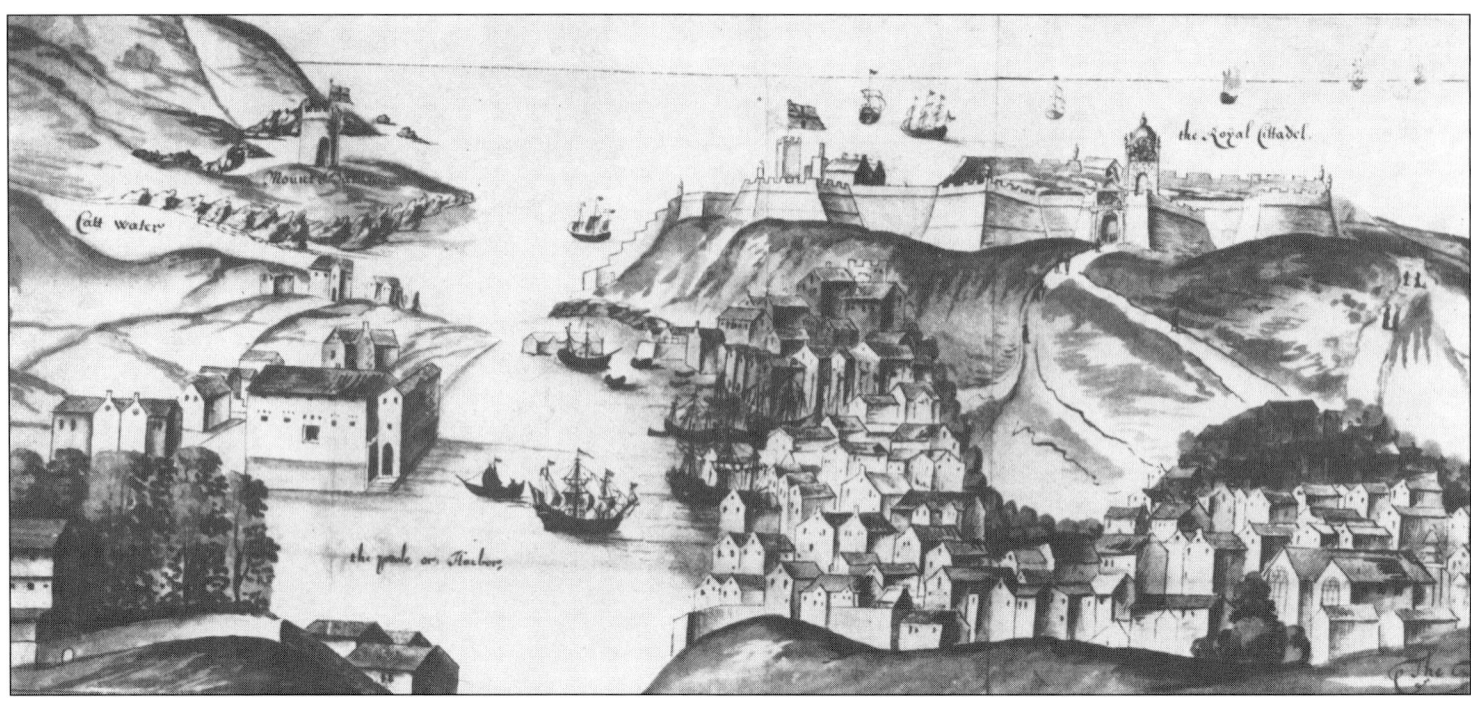

A drawing by Sir Bernard de Gomme, the engineer who built the Royal Citadel in 1666. Note how the Citadel dominates the town and harbour. The Fish House was in the harbour entrance (behind the ship) and the China House (left) was then part of a group of warehouses.

THE STUARTS

Like most seaports, Plymouth declared for Parliament in the Civil War. It withstood a royalist seige for three years, and only for a short time was the harbour out of use, when Mount Batten was occupied by the enemy. Even then, at the worst hours when the townsmen were starving, a 'miraculous draught of fishes' came into the Pool, so thick that people could scoop them up in baskets. One of the first things done at the end of the Civil War was to build a new defence for Sutton Harbour. Probably in 1651-2 a round tower of stone, capable of taking ten guns on the roof, was built opposite the harbour entrance. That is when the peninsula was first called Mount Batten, in honour of Captain Batten who had commanded Parliament's naval forces in the port during the war.

With the Restoration, King Charles II rebuilt Drake's Fort into the far bigger Citadel which still stands over the harbour. Some of the granite doorways from Drake's Fort were used again, notably the one in the wall facing the Sound, but the magnificent new gateway of the Citadel, sometimes but doubtfully ascribed to Wren, is one of the finest pieces of baroque architecture in the country.

Both Charles II and his brother James came down, twice, to see the Citadel being built. They were Plymouth's first yachtsmen, sailing down the Channel in the 'pleasure boat' *Henrietta*. They were also considering Plymouth's future as a naval base. Sutton Pool provided the base, Cattewater the off-anchorage: the Elizabethan fleets and Robert Blake's fleets in the Commonwealth had so used the port. But docks were needed for the King's ships in the Atlantic,

MILITARY USE

just as those at Portsmouth, Deptford, Woolwich and Chatham served the ships in the narrow seas. King Charles had Samuel Pepys, his principal civil servant at the Admiralty, with him. They landed at 5 p.m. on Monday 17 July 1671 at the Barbican Stairs; were up and out on the Hoe at four o'clock the next morning and then explored by boat the Hamoaze, the Cattewater and all round Sutton Pool. They dined the merchants of the town, and kissed their wives.

But neither Charles nor James were to build the Dock at Plymouth. When William of Orange landed in Brixham to oust James from the throne, his fleet came round to the Cattewater and the Citadel was the first fortress in England to surrender. Within three years King William started the building of Plymouth Dock on the Hamoaze (although the Cattewater had been the first choice) and Sutton Pool was no longer a naval base.

FEEDING THE NAVY

It did, however, remain the naval supply base. Arrangements for feeding the Navy were formalised when Cromwell set up Commissioners of Victualling in 1656. They were renting land for storehouses at Lambhay very soon after, for it was bought by the Crown in 1667 to make way for the Citadel. A naval storehouse was then acquired at Coxside, which served until the end of the French War of 1689-97 and was then turned over to the Board of Ordnance as a gunwharf. Eight years later a Victualling Office was set up at Lambhay again. The 'King's Bakehouse' remained at Coxside. It was burnt down, destroying many stores, in 1744 but rebuilt, and enlarged, the next year.

In 1750 this bakehouse was replaced by a new one at Lambhay and in 1756 the Commissioners for Sick and Wounded took over premises at Coxside. These would have been superseded when the Naval Hospital opened at Stonehouse in 1761, but 'shed prisons' for prisoners-of-war were set up about this time at Coxside.

From the sequence of usages, which never overlap, one might assume that all these references are to one set of buildings, and four clues suggest that they are what is now called the China House, originally built by a man called Rattenbury in 1654. First, they are always called 'storehouses' on old maps, a term not used for any other of the buildings round the harbour, and which might be a shortened form of 'naval store houses'. Secondly, there is a tradition that Marrowbone Slip, alongside the China House, got its name because the beef was boned before being put in casks, and the bones then thrown on the beach to be picked clean by seagulls—which again suggests a victualling yard. Thirdly, a Sutton Harbour map of 1757 describes these stores as a 'hospital for sick and hurt seamen'. Fourthly, the Shepherds, woollen manufacturers, rented warehouses at Coxside, certainly near this site, which later housed prisoners of war. Arthur Stert, MP for Plymouth on and off from 1734 to 1750, actually paid the rent for 26 years for Shepherd, so it is tempting to date this occupancy in the early part of the century when only the King's Bakehouse was there. It would be wrong to place too much reliance on Shepherd having used this block; there were three 'shed prisons' at Coxside, only replaced when Princetown Prison was opened in 1806.

The old block on Lockyer's Wharf also has an oral tradition of use by French prisoners of war. This building was erected, from map evidence, between 1757 and 1765, at the time when these prisons were ordered, so may well have been built for the purpose. Donne's 1765 map shows

SUTTON HARBOUR

The limestone gateway, suspected to have been built for an eighteenth-century prisoner of war camp, is now rebuilt in front of the multi-storey car park on Lockyer's Quay.

the block with a jetty in front, now under the wharf, and the buildings had a front wall of limestone with a large central archway and two flanking doorways, reminiscent of Crown building of this period and certainly too grand, even in its modern dilapidation, for plain commercial work. The building was demolished to make way for the multi-storey car park in 1995 but the gateway was rebuilt in front of the car park, serving no purpose and looking rather lost.

At the new Victualling Office at Lambhay, in the shadow of the Citadel, the new bakery and other premises were built about 1750, just to the right of the road that curves down to Commercial Wharf. The storehouses ran from the Barbican gateway to Fisher's Nose, with the granaries nearest the town, then the wine and spirit cellars, then the beef, pork, cheese and butter stores, and finally the lofts filled with biscuits. The warehouses grouped round Commercial Wharf survived until the 1930s; the wharf itself is unchanged. Of the storehouses only the building now used as the Mayflower Sailing Club headquarters survives.

All this had to be well guarded. There was no approach from the Barbican. The only road went past the Citadel gate and the warder's lodge, past the house and garden of the chief officer, and the offices of the agent victualler, the storekeeper, and the clerk of the cheque, to reach the stores. The brewery was at Millbrook.

From Blake to Nelson the English fleets drew provisions here, but the system and the swindles were as rotten as the stores issued. Admiral Hawke once complained that Lambhay bread was full of weevils and maggots, and the stores 'employ the whole time of the squadron in surveying it and throwing it overboard'. In fact one of the first ships built at Plymouth Dock, the *Looe*, was wrecked on the Irish coast when she tried to make port to replace the rotten stores from Lambhay which the crew could not eat.

When King George III toured the Victualling Office in August 1789 he had a cask broken open and a piece of the meat sent to Saltram, where he was staying, for him to taste. His verdict is not recorded.

Napoleon's brother Lucien was another famous man who landed in the old Victualling Office; he arrived there in 1810 to seek asylum at a time when he had fallen out with his brother. Not until the Royal William Victualling Yard was built at Stonehouse after the Napoleonic Wars did Sutton Harbour cease to provision the royal ships.

PRESS GANGS

Along with the ships' boats appearing on their peaceful missions to draw rations, Sutton Pool's naval visitors in the eighteenth and nineteenth centuries included press gangs. Only seamen were supposed to be pressed, while apprentices, freeholders, men under eighteen and over fifty-five were all protected from impressment. It was

MILITARY USE

never easy in a waterside town like Plymouth for a man to prove he was not a seaman however.

The worst 'hot press' of all was in 1803, when secret word was sent to Admiral Dacres, the commander-in-chief at Mount Wise, that war was to be renewed with the French. All leave for servicemen was stopped; the town was surrounded at nightfall by troops and then the press gangs moved in, armed with stretchers from the bottom of boats. Battles raged up and down the lamplit streets running down to the harbour, through every inn and tavern, as men were seized and hauled off to the ships. The able-bodied men who escaped the first descent went into hiding; even the ferries ceased to run. For days the town was in a state of seige, only relaxed as it was drained of men and the press gangs moved out to the country districts. The savagery of this press was long remembered in the popular ballad of the day *Sweet Poll of Plymouth*, about a girl whose sweetheart was torn from her.

> *And have they torn my love away.*
> *And is he gone ? she cry'd.*
> *My love, the sweetest flower in May.*
> *Then languished, drooped, and died.*

The verses are even engraved on a jug preserved in the City Museum.

Captain Lord Cochrane, needing men for his new ship, the *Pallas*, late in 1804, used the low trick of a press gang on Christmas Day. Falling foul of the law he was summoned to appear before the Mayor for wounding two constables. As autocratic as he was eccentric, he sent his reply:

> *Sir. I received your letter of yesterday's date this day at 12 o'clock. If anyone has cause of complaint let the due course of law be followed.*
> *Sir, your obedient servant,*
> *Cochrane.*

When he did not appear in court he was held to be in contempt, and a warrant issued for his arrest. By that time he was at sea; when he returned he and his crew had made a fortune in prize money and Cochrane never again had trouble in finding men. But the case dragged on through the High Courts for nearly two years, and though Plymouth won the case the town never seems to have recovered all its costs.

Even after the naval base moved to Hamoaze, Sutton still needed defending. Plymouth spent £88 on batteries at Pigg's Point and Mount Batten in 1690, when the French fleet came into view. Soon after 1700 a permanent battery was established at Pigg's Point. It was named Queen Anne's Battery, in honour of the new sovereign and, though one can only just trace the half-moon curve of the battery in front of the present marina, the name remains for the point of rocks. Some old engravings still show the crenellated semi-circular wall with its fourteen guns.

ROYAL MARINES

Regiments raised for sea service have been quartered in Plymouth since they were first raised in 1664. When these Marine regiments were put on a regular footing in 1775 and fifty companies of Marines were formed, the 3rd or Plymouth Division was entirely billeted in the town round the harbour. The orderly room was in the limestone building in Southside Street, between Southside Ope and Parade Ope. The first court martial was held in the Prince George Tavern at 14 Vauxhall Street, and parades were held on what was then the New Quay but which has been called the Parade ever since. Apart from ceremonial drills it was also the muster point if the alarm was raised. Not till 1783 did the Royal Marines move into their barracks at Stonehouse.

An eighteenth-century jug inscribed with the verses of Sweet Poll of Plymouth *and a picture of the stricken girl waving goodbye to the ship carrying away her press-ganged lover.*

SUTTON HARBOUR

An aerial view of the harbour in 1947. Craft of the Water Transport Company, Royal Army Service Corps, are clustered around the base of Sutton Jetty; a landing craft is being broken up off the China House in front of which are the boat-building slips of Shilston's Yard, revived in the Second World War to build small wooden vessels.

A variety of regiments have been housed in the Citadel at different times, which was also the seat of the Governor of Plymouth until a house (now Admiralty House) was built for him at Mount Wise in 1791. Frequently it was garrisoned by the Royal Regiment of Invalids, wearing the uniform still sported by the Chelsea Pensioners. A witness in the Cochrane case was a soldier of the Royal Veteran Battalion.

Since 1896 the Citadel has been manned by units of the Royal Artillery and since 1971 it has been 29 Commando Regiment, Royal Artillery, working as part of the Commando Brigade, Royal Marines. Plymouth bestowed the Freedom of the City on the Regiment in 1996.

In 1917 a seaplane station was founded at Mount Batten and continued on and off until the end of the flying boat era. It was busiest in the Second World War when the Royal Australian Air Force operated Sunderland flying boats from the base. Lawrence of Arabia spent much of his Air Force service at Mount Batten developing the fast motor launches whose descendants became the air-sea rescue craft, and the modern launches and target towers of the RAF which still operate out of the Cattewater. There was a water transport company of the War Department Fleet in the harbour until a year or two after the last war. The Americans had a landing craft base at Queen Anne's Battery from whose ramps many men sailed for the Normandy beaches in 1944.

Now Sutton Harbour, which has seen so many warriors, so many armies, so many fighting fleets, is given over to peace. But the scars in its old streets, the gaps where the ancient houses were destroyed in the German raids of the last war, show how Plymouth is still paying the price of Admiralty, as it did first in 1337.

CHAPTER 3
FISHING

When the first Plymouth man had tilled his farm he went fishing. When he had more fish than his family could eat he was in business. To keep fish it had to be salted, and salt could only be obtained in such quantities from the Biscay shores of France where the sun was warm enough to evaporate sea water from shallow pans on the beach, leaving the salt. The French had wine as well as salt to sell and were happy to buy salt fish. Sutton Harbour was in this trade long before Edward I came down with his soldiers; indeed the King only came because Sutton men and their ships were veterans of the passage round Ushant.

Plymouth had its own rich fishing ground just inside the Eddystone, where hake is the speciality. In medieval times all hake brought into Sutton Harbour paid a special due to maintain the old four-towered castle; castle hake they were called. When Drake's Fort was being built the Crown tried to pay for it by a special levy on all pilchards exported from Devon and Cornwall, but it was a hard struggle to collect the money. In any case Sutton Harbour's pilchard trade was being stolen from 1590 onwards by the merchants who built cellars and curing places from Cawsand round to Portwrinkle, where the fishermen had bases close to the fishing ground and cut out the three-mile sail across the Sound to land their catch.

Always fishermen reach out further and further for the richest, less depleted grounds. East Coast men were off to Iceland as early as the twelfth century. John Cabot came back to Bristol in 1497 to tell of untold wealth of fish off the 'new-found land' and within a short time the south Devon fishermen were sailing out across the Atlantic. Geographically they were well-placed to exploit these grounds, as the East Coast men had been the Arctic waters. Plymouth accounts refer to the Newfoundland men as early as 1543. By then the rich fishing grounds of Torbay were yielding four times as much local fish to Brixham, Paignton and Marychurch as Sutton was taking, so the new trade was a godsend to Plymouth and its tradition of bigger ships.

The Danes placed an embargo on the English fishing off Iceland at the end of the century, which opened the English markets to Newfoundland fish even more, and gave Plymouth and Dartmouth (its great rival in the trade) an enormous advantage. Their fleets trebled in size.

ACROSS THE ATLANTIC

The ships sailed from Sutton and the other west harbours on March 1, normally vessels of about a hundred tons with a crew of about forty men. They came home at the end of September: Plymouth records show fifty Newfoundland craft in port in the autumn of 1595, with two million fish aboard and Dutch and French merchants waiting to buy them. At that time the war with Spain was still in full cry and had given the Devon men an excuse to clear all foreign fishermen off the Grand Banks. By the end of the war in 1603 most ships were sailing their cargoes straight to Spain or Portugal at the end of the season to a ready market.

From 1615 onwards, when the banks had been fished for a century, new grounds were opened off the 'maine' of north America. Plymouth merchants set up fishing bases in the islands off the coast, as they had in Newfoundland, and fishermen could make three times as much money off New England as off Newfoundland. A 1630 writer says that one could often see a hundred sail of the fishing fleet at Plymouth, sometimes two hundred.

In 1641, just before the outbreak of the Civil War, Plymouth declared that it was chiefly dependent on the fish trade. But as the colony of Massachusetts grew from 1630 onwards so did the English fishermen lose those grounds, and the Civil War really put an end to the English fishing on the New England coast.

The shut down of this business, and the seige of Plymouth, hit the port badly. Whereas in 1631 it was sending sixty ships across the Atlantic, which means about 2400 men compared with Dartmouth's eighty, in 1652 Plymouth had only five ships out against Dartmouth's thirty-four. The trade recovered towards the end of the century but new methods required more capital. The richer merchants of London and Exeter were taking over, and Plymouth's share gradually fell away until it was down to a dozen ships by 1700. It was a less profitable trade, however, than in its early days (in the mid-century Plymouth and Dartmouth men in the business reckoned they were losing six per cent a year). The men of Sutton Pool were finding straight trade across the Atlantic more profitable, and the new Dockyard was opening fresh opportunities.

TURNPIKES AND RAILWAYS

The inshore fishermen of Sutton Harbour had a new fillip when the turnpike roads in the mid-eighteenth century made communication with the rest of England easier. This local fishing had never ceased. W. G. Maton in his *Observations on the Western Counties* of 1794-6 said Plymouth had 'a great exportation of pilchards to Italy and other Catholic countries'. In 1796 William Marshall's *Rural Economy of the West of England* reported 'the market of Plymouth has long, I believe, been esteemed the first in the island for the abundance, variety, and excellency of its sea fish. Of late years, however, this market has been worse supplied, as the prime fish caught by the fishermen in its vicinity, have been contracted for, by dealers, for that of Bath. And some share of the finny treasure, which these shores produce, is sent, I understand to the London market.'

Trawling started at about this time with Brixham the pioneer; and by 1820 there were thirty sailing trawlers working out of Sutton Pool. Then the railways gave the harbour a boost. Plymouth was connected by main line with London by 1848, twenty years before a branch line reached Brixham.

By 1850 Sutton Harbour had sixty trawlers in its fleet of eighty fishing boats, with another two or three hundred craft coming in for the pilchard and mackerel season. In one day alone half a million mackerel were brought in and sold for about £2000. In the first twelve days of March 1850 nearly 400 tons of mackerel was dispatched by rail. By 1862 nearly 2000 tons of fish was sent off by rail, and by 1872 there were sixty-six first class trawlers averaging 34 tons. Plymouth had

FISHING

A busy morning on the Barbican before the fish market was built in the 1890s. The trawlers were all sailing craft and so crowded that they berthed bows-on to the quay wall. The business of the market stretches from West Pier to the Navy Inn.

usurped Brixham's place as Devon's major fishing port.

All this fish was handled on the Barbican, for by law the only permitted wholesale fish market was in Sutton Harbour. The trade doubled between 1878 and 1888. In exceptional times there would be 300 fishing boats in harbour, and 400 or 500 handcarts on the quay waiting to handle the catches. One Lowestoft merchant bought £1000 worth of fish there a week. More fish came from Cornish ports by rail into Millbay, and other fishing boats landed there to avoid the congestion (and the dues) of Sutton Harbour; all of which was brought through the streets of the town by handcart. The Sutton Harbour men who paid their £1 a year resented what they called GWR fish, and on one occasion, in something like a riot, it was all thrown into the harbour. The fishermen could be rough customers too. A fight developed into such proportions one night that the Mayor, as chief magistrate, went down with the constables. He boarded one fishing boat whose crew promptly cast off the lines and began sailing him out through the pierheads. Order was eventually restored and the Mayor set safely ashore.

The Barbican then was a narrow quay barely thirty paces from the front of the houses to the water's edge. A line of cobbles parallel to the houses and laid at right angles to the others still marks the old sea wall. All the shipping agents, the railway companies, the fish merchants and the like had their offices on the quay, to add to the confusion, and something like 4000 people a year embarked at West Pier for ships in the Cattewater and the Sound. Often of a morning their cabs could get no further than the Navy Inn, where

SUTTON HARBOUR

The Barbican fish market in 1908. Even in those days it always attracted visitors such as the fashionable lady here with her children.

whole families would have to dismount, find a porter for their luggage, and battle as best they could over the cobbles between the piles of fish, the shouting auctioneers and the packed buyers, the fishermen and the porters, the handcarts and the buckets.

NEW FISH MARKET

So in 1889 the Sutton Harbour Improvements Company secured an Act of Parliament entitling them to build a new fish market. The company had discussed it for years, and Plymouth Corporation had gone so far as to have plans drawn up to build a fish market on Commercial Wharf. It came to nothing because the fishermen wanted to be inside the harbour piers. When the Improvement Company sought its Bill the Corporation actually opposed it, on the grounds that such revenues ought not to accrue to private profit, but be used to reduce the tolls on the fishermen. The Corporation even persuaded the House of Lords to incorporate into the final Act a clause that Plymouth should have the right to buy out the new market as soon as the company had built it, but the town did not exercise its option and the time limit ran out many years ago. The Great Western Railway also entered the lists against the Bill, but they appeared as plain straightforward business rivals.

The new Act renewed the company's authority to buy the harbour, which marked a vast step forward and because the market was built out over the bed of the harbour, in front of the Barbican, it was on company land whereas before the company had been renting the quay from the Corporation, and been getting back in return less revenue than they were paying out.

The new market was not actually opened until 1 February 1896 and an extension of time had to be obtained from Parliament. While building operations were in progress the Parade was used for the fish auctions and that led to a new row. Because there was only earth, not cement, between the cobbles there, the fish slime soaked down into the earth, and not only produced an abominable smell but entered the storm-water chamber under the Parade and built up so much sewer gas that the manhole covers were forced up. A ventilator on the Parade, later carrying a lamp on top, was an expedient to deal with the nuisance, and survived as a memorial to the temporary 1893-5 fish market.

The new fish market was built not just to meet the complaints about congestion in the old, but also to meet a new fishing boom. In 1885 Plymouth sent 3598 tons of fish away by rail, in 1890 the figure was 5159 tons. The 1886 value was £84 851, the 1890 value £162 900, with more fish to the value of £13 000 coming by rail from the Cornish ports to the Plymouth market. No wonder the handcarts from Millbay to Sutton were a nuisance. The peak year was 1892 with 7352 tons of fish landed. But already the industry was changing - steam trawling had started in the North Sea, resulting in vast catches which not only began to put the sailing smacks out of business but increasingly led to the concentration of the industry in a few large ports. It also meant over-fishing in the North Sea and by the turn of the century the new steam trawlers were reaching back to the rich and historic Arctic grounds. The first locally owned steam trawler, the *Reginald* arrived in 1896. She had a red funnel abaft the wheelhouse. Within a decade there were five locally-owned steam trawlers and the firm of Chant & Paddon had been specially formed to operate them.

Sail trawling out of Plymouth was beginning to fail. The boom was over. By 1900 the value of fish landed was cut back to £101 000 and by 1904 was down to £72 000. The fishing industry was described as distressed. It is of course an industry that depends on the supply of fish in the sea; if the fish is not there all the efforts and the capital spent are to no avail, and fish are migratory creatures of changing habits. Chant & Paddon had built their own coal store and maintenance depot on the end of Bayly's Wharf, across the harbour, but they complained that the Sutton Harbour Company had let a coal firm build a big store right alongside which hampered their boats and their trade. The company was willing to build Chant & Paddon a special wharf for their exclusive use if they would double the number of their steam trawlers (at their height they had seven, but one was wrecked on the French coast). With the state of fishing the firm could not do this, and the deadlock remained until the outbreak of war in 1914.

With the rise of the steam trawlers fish became cheaper and more plentiful and the fish and chip shop was born. In turn their demand for cheap fish led to a new trade, and new problems, in Plymouth. Dogfish, which had been thrown overboard or given to the crew, and generally cursed as a nuisance, became marketable in Plymouth about 1905 and the small hookers which had previously been laid up in the winter months found it profitable to catch them by line. Over half a dogfish is thrown away and the offal problem in the market grew. The Plymouth Corporation had removed all fish waste until 1906 but, no doubt disturbed by the vast increase in quantities, then refused to move any more.

An enterprising character started the Plymouth Fish Guano & Oil Company in a waterside shed at Mount Batten, whence he carted the offal by barge, and by steam process made it into fertilizer. The smell with a southerly wind was so bad that complaints even came from Mutley, a mile

Plymouth's first steam trawler, the Reginald, *went aground on St Mary's in the Isles of Scilly in July 1902. She suffered no damage and her crew had a bite on the beach while waiting for high tide, when she was towed off and got home under her own steam. She had arrived in Plymouth in 1896.*

SUTTON HARBOUR

East Coast drifters in for the herring season; boxing the catch spread right along the quay, even past the old 'Iron Duke' lavatory for the men, now replaced by limestone conveniences.

away, and in 1912 an injunction shut down the factory. The Improvement Company also passed a by-law forbidding the gutting of fish in the market. But with forty to sixty hookers 'dogging' the by-law was not over-enforced, and the Batten factory was revived.

The 1914-18 war and its demands for food kept the trade going, especially important when Admiralty restrictions virtually limited fishing to close inshore. When the Admiralty took over Mount Batten in 1917 to set up a Royal Naval Air Station the guano factory finally went out of business. The Improvement Company had to enforce their 'no-gutting' by-law in self defence, and in December 1917 the fishermen refused to go to sea, saying they could not gut their fish afloat in their small boats. A compromise was reached, that the company would supply bins into which the men would gut on the quay, and they would take the bins to sea on their next trip and empty them.

GOING TO LAW

By 1919 there were 30 000 to 40 000 dogfish - or flake as they were now politely called - being landed on average every day through November to February, and the resulting offal was about twenty-five tons a day. The company tried to enforce its by-law which the fishermen refused to observe, and a test case was taken to the Plymouth magistrates.

Isaac Foot fought the fishermen's case and won, so the company appealed. The Lord Chief Justice, the great Lord Reading, sent the case back to the magistrates for more evidence, and as they examined possible alternatives to the fish market for gutting, Isaac Foot was ironically suggesting the use of Princess Square, the heart of the lawyer's quarter, and even Guildhall Square. Henry Turner appeared for the company and the chairman of the Plymouth magistrates was Lovell Dunstan, a Southside Street ship's chandler and later leader of the Council; quite a collection of Sutton Pool worthies. In January 1920 the Lord Chief Justice, sitting with Mr Justice Avory and Mr Justice Sankey and solemnly debating the time it took a man to clean a dogfish, found that the by-law was unreasonable. But there was also an injunction in Chancery, where Mr Justice Russell said he thought the by-law not unreasonable, but in view of the higher court's decision he would agree with them. This encouraged the company to go to appeal, and the Master of the Rolls finally found in their favour.

One effect of the new dogfish business of the prewar days was that the annual number of landings from sailing craft doubled, from 320 in 1907 to 654 in 1913, while the steam trawler landings fell away from 283 in 1909 to 179 in 1913. The war virtually stopped fishing from larger vessels and when a French trawler discharged a load of dog-

FISHING

An early photograph of fish laid out in the old market for auction, almost certainly pre-1914. The scene contrasts sharply with that in the present-day fish market.

fish in 1919 it was the first steam trawler to discharge in Sutton Harbour for three-and-a-half years. But the long rest had benefitted the fishing grounds. The stocks had built up during the war and the herring shoals, always uncertain migrants, were back. In the winter of 1919-20 there were a hundred steam and motor drifters working out of Plymouth, in from Yarmouth, Lowestoft and the Cornish ports. In one night half a million fish were landed, including 40 000 mackerel and some dogfish.

BOOM YEARS

For the next ten years Plymouth catches increased steadily, until by 1930 Plymouth handled more fish than Newlyn, which had been the premier Westcountry fishing port since the turn of the century. The trawl and line catches remained fairly constant, but the drifters catching pilchards, mackerel and herring, showed the real improvement. In the winter of 1927-28 there were seventy-seven East Coast drifters, as well as the Cornish fleet. The two months season yielded nearly 123 000 cwt of herring, three times as much as the trawler yield of 39 000 cwt for the whole year. Special trains were chartered to carry the herring, and the German and Dutch trawlers were 'klondiking', exporting the fresh fish to Europe.

Scottish and East Coast 'herring lassies' were brought down year after year to deal with the fish on the quayside, and some of them kippered the herring over fires of mahogany chips in a store at the back of New Street. There are some lively tales told about them.

The peak year was 1930 when 24 000 crans were landed, valued at £66 000. Thereafter a

SUTTON HARBOUR

Another herring season, c. 1930, with Lowestoft drifters lying double-banked at the quay.

steady decline set in, broken only by one good year in 1932. The western men spotted the decline before the East Coast men; 1931 saw 177 Cornish boats fishing out of Plymouth but after that year their numbers fell away to a handful. On the other hand the East Coast drifters using the port increased in number each year up to the record of 105 in 1936, but the catch that year was only half what the visiting fifty-four East Coast drifters in 1930 shared. But they took the point; next year only fifty-six East Coast boats came down, in 1938 only three, and they have not been seen since.

From 1919 to 1930 the trawl fishing remained fairly static, with peak years in 1931 and 1933. In 1938 Sutton Harbour was the base of thirteen steam trawlers, its largest steam fleet ever. Mr J. G. Wilson owned the *Trojan* and *Oakwold*, both built on the East Coast in the 1890s; Percy Turner owned the *Condor*, Plymouth Trawlers Ltd (Mr John Chant was a director, and the firm in direct descent from the pre-war Chant & Paddon) owned *Sea Hawke, Dereske, Eastbourne* and *Atlantic*; Sanders Stevens owned *Stormcock* and *Verity*, and Mr W. Nicholls the *Elk*. A new company, Plymouth Mutual Steam Fishing Co., was formed with Mr W. J. W. Modley, of Bigwood's Ice Factory, as chairman. They bought three more trawlers in Hull which Plymouth Trawlers Ltd managed for them. But the smacks were disappearing fast; the 1930 fleet of seventeen had fallen to six by 1931 and after 1937 there was only one in the port. She too went out of commission with the outbreak of war.

Fishing kept up reasonably well for the duration, with the hooker fleet only falling from forty-two boats in 1939 to twenty-nine by 1945. For most of the war years there were seven steam trawlers in the port, but as they had killed the sailing smacks, so the new diesel motor craft were to put them out of business. The steamers slowly disappeared with the last one, Percy Turner's *Perverus*, fishing her last season in 1954. She was the last steam trawler on the South Coast.

During the war the Admiralty had designed and built a large fleet of what they called motor fishing vessels, MFVs, as maids of all work. When they were released at the end of the war they altered not only the motive-power but the appearance of the fishing fleets, resembling neither the old steamers nor the traditional smacks, killing the local traditions in fishing boat designs and substituting a single pattern across the whole country. They did not keep the monopoly, however, and the appearance of the Plymouth fleet today is as varied as it ever was.

POST-WAR PROBLEMS

But a long decline set in. The 37 500 cwt of fish landed in 1947 was just about the same as the trawler landings of twenty years before. By 1963,

Sailing trawlers tied up alongside the old fish market.

although the number of large fishing boats actually had increased from six to eight, the catch was down to 8000 cwt. In spite of the rise in money values, the 1963 catch only yielded £44 000 against the £89 000 of 1947. Then a slow recovery began. By 1968 the catch had increased by fifty per cent to 12 500 cwt valued at £82 000, and there were fourteen first-class boats at work. During this time the proportion of the catches of the western ports had changed. Newlyn which had been a little higher in 1947 was showing treble the Plymouth figure by 1968, and Brixham, which had begun to overtake Plymouth in the late 1930s, was landing double the amount in 1968. One vital development in Plymouth, however, was the shell-fishing, which between the wars was still left to the fishing villages. In 1947 Plymouth shell fish were worth £3000, but by 1968 this had risen to £23 500, in addition to the wetfish returns. So the total value of fish landings, wet and shell, for 1968, amounted to £105 105.

But a real boom came after 1967, when British territorial waters were extended from three to twelve miles. This kept the big Russian fishing fleets as well as the individual Frenchmen and Belgians off the valuable inshore grounds. At the same time Sutton Harbour spent £25 000 on

SUTTON HARBOUR

The steam trawler Roskeen *alongside the Barbican in January 1928.*

Mending nets in the 1960s.

improving the fish market services. Diesel fuel became available alongside and Bigwoods (Plymouth Cold Store Ltd), ice merchants in the port since 1789, installed a new ice plant in a building especially constructed by the Sutton Harbour company, from which ice was tipped by shute straight into the holds. So the turn-round of the fishermen was speeded, and a new range of offices for the fish salesmen and the Ministry of Agriculture and Fisheries replaced the old wooden huts. The market remained structurally the same, looking like a lost railway station under its Victorian roof, but it was geared for the boom.

Other factors helped. New gear was developed for catching pelagic fish - mackerel, pilchards and herring - and world markets were opening up for shellfish, not just crabs and lobsters but scallops and queen scallops. By 1974 there were 114 fishing vessels registered at Plymouth with another thirty craft over 40ft in the Plymouth-Cawsand fleet using Sutton Harbour exclusively. Even bigger vessels from Teignmouth, Brixham, the Channel Islands and Scotland worked out of the Pool for a long winter season, with smaller craft from other south Devon and Cornish ports. In 1975 Brixham & Torbay Fish Ltd, a fisherman's co-operative, took over the quayside ice plant and planned to expand production. To cope with the heavy landings more quay space had to be found, and pelagic fish - mainly mackerel - were landed at Bayly's Wharf and Lockyer Quay at Coxside, sometimes up to 300 tons a day. New suction methods emptied the holds at high speed. Live storage tanks for crabs and lobsters were also established there. The scallop landings led to fish processing factories being opened at Saltash and Buckfastleigh. In 1970 the Sutton Harbour company also bought Bigwood's old freezing plant in Citadel Ope, installed new deep freeze equipment, and a shellfish processing factory there exported their products to the United States and Europe.

Fish exports have developed considerably, partly through Britain's entry into the Common Market. Mackerel goes to France, Holland and Germany, pilchards to Belgium, bass and monk fish to France, crabs to Sweden, and most of the scallops and queens to the United States. In 1976 a new trawler joined the fleet, planning to catch horse mackerel for an African market.

In round figures the 12 000 cwt of pelagic fish landed at Plymouth in 1970 had risen to over 68 000 cwt in 1973 and leapt to 177 000 cwt by 1974. Shell fish landings of 1600 cwt in 1970 were over 29 000 in 1974. Against this Plymouth's handling of the more expensive demersal fish, such as plaice and sole, which remained fairly constant between 8000 and 9000 cwt in the early 1970s, fell to under 6000 cwt in 1974. So that while Plymouth was now landing in weight more fish than its old rivals, Newlyn and Brixham, put together, the total value of its catch was £389 000 against Newlyn's £877 000 and Brixham's £709 000. But Sutton Harbour was advancing faster than any other fishing port in the West. The provisional figures for 1975 showed 372 000 cwt, valued at £1.06 million, landed. Only Newlyn in the West showed a higher value. Scallops made nearly a third of the Sutton valuation figure.

There were over fifty shore workers in the trade on the Barbican alone, and all told the fishing out of Sutton Harbour employed up to 600 people. In the autumn of 1975 there were signs of the herring returning. The current boom had already passed in tonnage the previous peak of 1892 but fish come and go. Sutton Harbour had been stimulated by a boom in its oldest industry at a time of world depression.

CHAPTER 4
TRADE

Plymouth was born on the shores of Sutton Pool because of the natural excellence of the harbour, and its good land communications. Plymouth Sound is the only sheltered harbour between Dartmouth and Fowey (Salcombe's bar has always been its drawback), and while there are other harbours in the port of Plymouth, Sutton always came first. The oldest surviving customs record for the port, that of 1437, shows that Sutton had six ships, Saltash three, Landulph three, Stonehouse two, Millbrook one, and the Yealm one. Until Tudor times there was only a small population in the hinterland to buy imported goods and not much production to go out. There was tin from West Dartmoor from 1150 onwards, in fluctuating and never large quantities.

When the wool trade developed the main centres were on the Devon-Somerset border and Plymouth only dealt in the coarser cloth from Tavistock, with some of the Ashburton output. Apart from that there were slates, found in abundance in the shillety rocks behind Plymouth, hides from the cattle, and fish. Fetching salt from West France to cure fish took Plymouth into the Bordeaux wine trade early on, but more wine came into Plymouth than the local population was liable to drink. Plymouth ships brought around 200 000 gallons of wine out of Bordeaux in the autumn of 1308, at a time when the whole population of Devon was only about 72 000.

Plymouth was in a key situation at the west end of the Channel, a point where many sea routes meet. The first cargo recorded out of the port was in the year 1211 and consisted of bacon for Portsmouth and wine for Nottingham. The bacon could be a local product, but the wine is clearly a re-export being trans-shipped by coaster. From trade figures at the time of Richard II (1377-99) it is clear that there was not only much wine coming in but also a great deal of Baltic stores like hemp, pitch and canvas, used in shipbuilding. No doubt the wine ships took the Baltic goods back to Spain and Portugal, and the Baltic ships in turn took home wine. Special customs arrangements were made in Sutton Pool for this kind of exchange. Just as foreign ships were using Sutton, so ships from Sutton were trading away from their home port. Some carried wine direct to London, which because of its size, its wealth, and its position opposite Europe, dominated English commerce from the earliest times.

The Plymouth seamen, reaching round Ushant, were developing ocean experience and ships. To the wine business they added a virtual monopoly in the lucrative trade of carrying pilgrims to the shrine of St James of Compostello, or Santiago, in northern Spain. Some pilgrims went to Bordeaux and rode over the Pyrenees, some went on by sea to the ports of Northern Spain. Plymouth was licensed to trade with Portugal by 1362; and the 1437 customs books show her ships ranging from

SUTTON HARBOUR

A picture taken in 1965 showing the tower of St Andrew's church looking down on Sutton Harbour; the quays beneath it are probably the oldest in the harbour. The church tower was paid for by a Tudor merchant trading out of the port.

Norway to Italy. The piracy during the Wars of the Roses damaged lawful trade. As early as 1386 the English wine ships had assembled in Plymouth to sail round Brittany in convoy. Plymouth men played their full part in Channel piracy whenever the opportunity presented, as the records show from the fourteenth to the seventeenth centuries, but their profits are not shown in the statistics, and the legal trade which is recorded shows a fall in returns only partly due to the depredations. It is in any case difficult to get figures for one harbour like Sutton, because until the early sixteenth century all the English ports were lumped into eighteen groups, and the Plymouth-Fowey customs returns also include all the Cornish ports. But in 1465 this group was thirteenth in importance for its import-export figures, and by the end of the century Thomas Yogge had made enough money shipping Ashburton woollens from Plymouth to buy the materials for St Andrew's Church tower, which looks down on the harbour to this day.

ACROSS THE ATLANTIC

Then ocean trade changed. The Portuguese rounded the Cape of Good Hope in 1487. Columbus crossed the Atlantic in 1492. The accession of Henry VII in 1485 brought firm government and a rapid cut in Channel piracy. The western wool industry began to grow apace, and with it the population.

The weight of English trade began to shift from the North Sea to the Atlantic seaboard where Plymouth men had the lead already. By 1520 Plymouth-Fowey had moved up to eleventh place, and one family, the Eliots of Plymouth, made a fortune shipping Ashburton wool and Cornish tin and bought the priory of St Germans at the Dissolution of the Monasteries. The family is still there, ennobled as the Earls of St Germans.

A friend of John Eliot, William Hawkins (whose roots were in Tavistock, probably again wool and tin) led the way across the Atlantic. Although by 1543 he was the third richest man in Plymouth with all his capital in the Spanish trade, he sailed personally in command of his 250 ton *Paule of Plymouth*, which made the first trading voyage across the Atlantic of any English ship. Hawkins brought ivory on the African coast and brazil wood (for drying cloth) on the South American coast, and the trade was established. The voyages became regular annual affairs, and one alone in 1540 paid off a thousand per cent on capital invested. Twenty years later, in 1562, his son John Hawkins extended the business by buying slaves in Africa and trading them in Spanish American ports for pearls, sugar, ginger and hides. Spain resented intruders in her colonies and from this in part grew the Spanish wars which lasted till the end of Elizabeth's reign. But Englishmen were established as transatlantic traders and from this business came Drake's voyage round the world. Again it started and finished in Sutton Pool, but it also opened up to English ships the riches of the East Indies, and led eventually to the formation of the East India Company and the Indian empire.

By 1614-20 Plymouth had risen to sixth place among English ports. Customs returns for these years show the distribution of trade. London averages about £112 000 to £120 000. Then comes a sharp drop to the outports, Hull, £7300; Exeter, £4500; Bristol, £3700; Newcastle, £3300; Plymouth £2900; followed by Lyme Regis, Southampton and Dartmouth, in that order. Plymouth's best return of £3462 in 1617 actually took her to fifth place, above Newcastle. Yet altogether Exeter had a larger trade than Plymouth, because she was closer to the biggest wool-producing area. Plymouth had more American trade, however, and later in the century Exeter was sending serges in coasters to Sutton Pool for export to America. In return the coasters were taking goods from Spain, Ireland and America back to Exeter.

For the last quarter of the seventeenth century Plymouth slowly rose from sixth to fifth place, her customs returns increasing from £14 000 in 1672 to nearly £20 000 in 1687. London, Bristol, Hull and Exeter were the generally superior ports, with Dover, Southampton, Newcastle, Yarmouth and Cowes jostling for the lower places. But London as ever was sucking in the trade of the provincial ports, taking the Indies and much of the American business. Plymouth had lost her tobacco trade from Virginia by 1700 but the old business with Spain, Portugal and the Atlantic islands were left to her. Even here London was all-demanding, for although in 1686 Plymouth was the fourth port in the country in this trade, her share was only one-eighth that of London. Plymouth maintained these trading links right into this century, but it stayed small beer. In the seventeenth and eighteenth centuries the Channel was a battlefield between England and France, a hunting ground for the Algerine pirates, and this with the shift of industry to the Midlands and the North helped Bristol and Liverpool as much as anything. Naval needs became paramount at Plymouth very early; even though Sutton Harbour kept its trade and the weekly assembly of convoys for much of the eighteenth century brought business to all the boatmen, shipbrokers and the like. The Navy disliked anchored merchantmen getting in their way in the Sound and a 1747 order was they should get into harbour, or be prosecuted.

The press-gang also damaged trade. Worth in his *Plymouth* quotes an old man who could remember the mid-eighteenth century when 'the Parade was full of hogsheads of sugar, rum, rice, tobacco, and every colonial produce, the property of the merchants, particularly the great Mr Morshead, the leading man of the Corporation. War breaking out put a stop to all commercial enterprise... Wealth flowing in from the lucrative channel of prizes and prize goods without hazards, the foreign pursuits are soon forgotten, and being a King's Port, on the first impress the seamen fly to London, Bristol and Liverpool'.

GROWING TRADE

But although 42 years of the eighteenth century saw England at war, Sutton Pool's trade was actually bigger at the end of the century than at the beginning. While foreign trade inevitably fell off in wartime it never died; even the wine trade was maintained right through the Seven Years War and there were regular landings in those mid-century war years of corn and flour, coal, wine and spirits, salt, tobacco and wool. The wars meant that Devonport grew very fast, and Plymouth to a

SUTTON HARBOUR

The Jewish cemetery, close to the United Services public house on Citadel Green.

Opposite: The Elizabethan House in New Street and immediately above it the Palace Vaults, built in 1809 to cope with the influx of prize goods during the Napoleonic Wars.

lesser degree; the coastwise coal trade doubled between 1730 and 1760, and had doubled yet again by the end of the century, totalling about 90 000 tons a year. House-building too stepped up the timber demand, and there is a big jump in the timber imports of the 1760s.

The number of Queen Anne and later eighteenth-century houses which can still be found round the harbour are a testimony to the wealth of the day. Probably the most successful merchants in these colonial days were the Rogers family. They had been raised to the baronetcy in 1698, were the first family in the town to own a coach, and in the late nineteenth century Sir F. L. Rogers became Lord Blachford. The title lapsed on his death, and the only reminder of the once great family is the Dame Hannah Rogers School, now at Ivybridge but founded by her at 'Bowling Green' (Bedford Place), North Hill. Further proof that money could be made in eighteenth-century Plymouth is the Synagogue of 1762 in Catherine Street, built by the Jews who originally came to peddle their wares round the ships and settled close to the harbour. Their cemetery lies behind the houses at the top of New Street.

In the Napoleonic War came frantic activity, for Plymouth was the major port for the auctioning of prizes and their cargoes. It was said that one could walk from Sutton Harbour to Turnchapel over the decks of the prizes, so thick were they; and Captain Lord Cochrane (who had the press gang troubles with the Mayor in 1804) brought in the *Pallas* in 1806 with three great gold church candlesticks, captured en route from Mexico to Spain, one lashed to each masthead. At one time Cochrane brought so much captured claret into the Cattewater that the price fell away to less than the duty. So Cochrane, who had melted the candlesticks down rather than pay duty, poured the wine into the tide.

The Plymouth merchants were fully occupied as agents for London, Liverpool and Bristol houses, buying the prize goods and shipping them off. From February 1793 to September 1801 there were 948 prize ships 'examined' in the port, apart from others examined at sea before arrival. People were flocking in to share Plymouth's prosperity, and the town had its first real expansion since the spacious Elizabethan days. Great limestone warehouses grew up all round Sutton Pool to store the prize goods. One in New Street for instance has a plaque inscribed 'J. G. Werninck,

Palace Vaults, 1 September 1809', and in Vauxhall Street a brick-fronted warehouse (now vanished) was dated 1805. By 1813 there were 110 registered prize stores round the harbour.

With the end of the war came the inevitable collapse. Men were set to build the road under the Hoe as an unemployment relief scheme, and there were bread riots with drawn swords in Treville Street. But the merchants and professional men of Plymouth at the time were both hard-headed and long-sighted; they had foreseen what would happen, and formed the Port of Plymouth Chamber of Commerce as early as 1813. It was housed in the Exchange in Vauxhall Street, built in 1813 as a centre of trade. The Plymouth Marine Insurance Company was there as well. As early after the war as December 1815 three ships were sent off to revive the West Indies trade.

The Plymouth, Devonport, Portsmouth, and Falmouth Steam Packet Company was formed in 1822, and six years later the South Devon Shipping Company came into being.

By the 1830s there was not only a steady West Indian trade but a timber trade with North America, the Baltic, and the Mediterranean, a strong coastal trade and upwards of 350 vessels, totalling 30 000 tons, belonging to the port. Many anchored in the Cattewater, and 'at the western pier of the Barbican a great number of watermen ply for hire, but as they are not under particular regulations, persons employing them make the best bargains they can'. Their successors are still there, running the motor boats to Cawsand and the 'Four Rivers and Dockyard' excursions. Tolls received from shipping by the new Sutton Harbour Company tell their own story. In the first complete year, 1813, the figure was £1069. The last year of the war, 1815, produced £1713 but this figure was not surpassed until the £1835 of 1828. The next two years just passed the £2000 mark, and then there was a recession through the 1830s and recovery in the 1840s, to a figure of £2363 by 1846. The Industrial Revolution, and the rapid growth of population in England, produced a great upsurge in the shipping business.

CUSTOM HOUSE

Proof of Plymouth's share in this still stands in the fine Custom House on the Parade, designed by David Laing with its five arches supported by rusticated piers and built in 1820. It is still the best formal building on the waterfront. The first Custom House in Plymouth still stands almost opposite the present Custom House, on the south side of the Parade. It was built in the 1580s and has the date on its granite lintel; now so worn as to be indecipherable. This was replaced by a larger establishment alongside the present building, behind what old maps call Custom House Quay.

The 1820 Custom House, still in use. In this picture, probably taken before the First World War, the store to the right housed 'H. Crocker, Customs and General Agent; Wine Merchants.'

SUTTON HARBOUR

The Elizabethan Custom House on the Parade in the 1890s, when it was a store for Harris, a wine merchant, according to the board over the entrance. It has since been restored and spent much of its days after the Second World War as a betting shop.

By 1800 this building was not only inconvenient but beginning to fall apart. After the Second World War the site became the car park between the Three Crowns and the Sutton Harbour office. The Elizabethan Custom House was for many years after the war a betting shop.

By 1850 *White's Directory* recorded 'there is now no port in the English Channel, between London and Land's End, where so great an amount of business is done as at Plymouth, and where so much shipping is employed'. There were consuls or vice-consuls for thirty nations. Registered in the port in 1849 were 433 vessels totalling 29 657 tons. The year before, 4106 vessels entered the port, totalling 399 798 tons, 538 from foreign ports, 175 from Ireland and 3393 coasting. Cleared with cargo were 2343, of which 105 went foreign, 328 in ballast, 236 to Ireland, 1585 coasting, and 89 emigrant ships (of which more later) with 8505 passengers. Customs duty had grown from £100 000 in 1838 to £121 000 in 1849, with a peak in 1841 of £135 000. Exports were copper and lead ores, manganese, granite, limestone, china clay and fish. Imports were chiefly wine, fruit, corn and timber, with coal from Newcastle and South Wales the main coastal import.

At this time Millbay became a real competitor, berthing three ships totalling 698 tons in 1848, and jumping to 910 ships of 195 000 tons within ten years. Millbay took the big ships, a new trade, without really biting into the Sutton Harbour figures. Except for one year Millbay handled more tonnage every year from 1851 onwards, but she did not handle more ships until 1861. In the same way the opening of the Cattewater by the railway in 1875 seems to have generated new trade; Millbay figures show a temporary recession but then resume their steady climb. Cattewater moved at once into second place, handling double the tonnage of Sutton Harbour. Yet Sutton did not lost its business; from handling 1335 ships of 77 000 tons in 1850 it was coping with 1230 ships of 87 000 tons in 1880; fewer but bigger craft.

In 1890, of the 5322 vessels which discharged or loaded cargoes in Plymouth, 2921 used Millbay, 1443 the Cattewater, and 958 Sutton Pool. Tonnages show that the Millbay ships averaged 200 tons, but the Sutton and Cattewater ships just over 100 tons. Up to the outbreak of the First World War Millbay steadily increased the tonnages of cargoes handled, but with rather fewer and larger ships. In the Cattewater the number of ships remained about the same, but their tonnage doubled. In Sutton Pool the number of ships fell steadily to 690 in 1903 but then leapt to 1582 in 1904 and only slowly dropped again to the 1000 mark by 1910. Ship sizes were increasing in Sutton too, but many of them were still very small craft. It is interesting to note that only about a third of the ships using Sutton Pool each year were steamers, the rest sail. In the peak year of 1904 there were only 304 steamers in Sutton against 1278 sailing craft. The last sailing ship to bring cargo into the pool was the Finnish barque *Alastor* in March 1937. Naturally enough the steamers were mainly bringing in coal, though some was still carried under sail. Westcott's little topsail schooners and brigs would take china clay to Runcorn and ship back Lancashire coal, mixing this with running across to Newfoundland for salt cod (one voyage as late as 1914) or down to the Mediterranean for fruit.

All the Plymouth quays were busier with imports than exports. Coming into Sutton Harbour in 1896, for example, were coal for the gas works and the householders, timber, blue lias, cement, pyrites, ice, codfish, corn, animal feeding stuffs, potatoes, salt, fruit, bricks, and manure. Exports were china clay, arsenic (from the copper mines) and coke.

TRADE

BETWEEN THE WARS

The 1914-18 war hit the coastal trade, and so Sutton Harbour, severely, but when business revived after the war it was bedevilled for a time in 1919 when the dockers went on strike and without coal the gas works nearly ran out of gas. Then, with the fall in money values, the harbour dues had to be increased, to everyone's discomfort.

But things recovered; by 1934 Sutton Harbour was handling 242 000 tons of imports and 7587 tons of exports, not much below the Millbay figures. The main imports were coal, timber, cement and potatoes, the main exports china clay and, oddly enough, ice. These figures remained fairly constant until the 1939-45 war, during which years the imports ran between 100 000 and 150 000 tons each year, and exports fell to negligible proportions. By 1950 the total figures had recovered to over the 200 000 ton mark, with coal the great import and coke from the gas works giving the export figures a lift.

One can take the 1960 returns to show Sutton's share of the trade of the port. The Pool handled 162 000 of the 266 000 tons of coal imported, 6000 of the 51 000 tons of timber imported, and altogether 180 789 of the 1 127 000 tons of imports, about a sixth. Of the exports Sutton had 12 188 of the total 186 000 tons, about one fifteenth, made up mostly of coke and spent oxide.

Plymouth's one real export is china clay, now entirely shipped from Victoria Wharfs in the Cattewater, and that has increased from 9000 tons in 1948 to a peak of 388 000 tons in 1974. The total exports have grown from 34 000 tons in 1947 to 513 000 tons in 1974. The main imports are coal, grain, fertilisers, timber, fruit and vegetables, with petrol showing the biggest increase, from 79 000 tons in 1947 to a peak of 978 000 tons in 1969, and has hovered round that figure since 1953. The figure is some half million tons higher than the import figures for 1880-90. As late as 1876 Plymouth was twelfth in the order of English ports; now in spite of considerable growth she has fallen out of the big port league altogether and the smallest port in the top twelve handles fifty times as much cargo as Plymouth. The port has grown but not on the scale of the others; as ships have got bigger so foreign trade has concentrated in a few big ports, and since the roads have savaged the trade both of the railways and the coastal shipping so even that business has gone. Nor is it Plymouth's fault that she did not keep pace with her rivals; apart from suffering from the railway war she has always been held back by the Admiralty who for two centuries saw commercial shipping in Plymouth as being in their way.

The Norwegian barque Mimosa *alongside Sutton Quay in March 1915. Note the potato conveyor left of what is now Dolphin House, and the railway wagons right on North Quay.*

45

SUTTON HARBOUR

The Finnish barque Alastor *on North Quay in March 1937; the last sailing ship to bring cargo into the harbour.*

The warehouse on Sutton Quay before it was converted into flats as Dolphin Court. It served many purposes: storing fruit, potatoes and animals feed, all of which was transported across the gantry.

The Cattewater has shown the biggest tonnages in and out of Plymouth for many years because it not only monopolises the export of Lee Moor china clay, but it also takes the bulk of the imported petrol and allied products. For some years Sutton Harbour also showed larger tonnages than Millbay, but this ended in 1969 when the South-Western Gas Board closed its old coal-using gas works at Coxside. Not only did this take 100 000 tons of coal from Sutton's import figures, but another 10 000 tons of coke from the exports. With the general recession of 1974-75 the overall trade of Plymouth showed a fall, with Cattewater suffering a heavy fall in oil imports and the Sutton Harbour's trade reduced almost entirely to the house coal coming in to Bayly's Wharf for Plymouth Coal Co. Ltd, a subsidiary of the Renwick Group. In the years from 1969 to 1974 the total tonnage handled in the port fell from 1 798 000 to 1 668 000, with Cattewater 's share falling from 1 453 000 to 1 360 000 and Sutton's figures dropping from 97 000 to 68 000.

In 1975 Sutton Harbour's total tonnage was down to 55 000 tons. The one move against the trend was Millbay's increase from 171 000 tons to 240 000 tons, a result of the cross-Channel ferry from Roscoff which a French company launched that year. It was so successful that a second ship was brought on the route in 1975, with both cars and passengers as well as the freight lorries the service was basically designed for.

But apart from coal and fertiliser imports, and steel turnings exported, Sutton Harbour's commercial trade languished. With the fish trade clamouring for more quay space and with the new yachting marina spreading fast, it might not be to the overall detriment of the harbour. But when Sutton Pool ceased to have all connection with mercantile shipping it was a sad break with a long and distinguished past.

One reminder of this past, the topsail schooner *Kathleen & May*, was berthed in Sutton Harbour, alongside Guy's Quay. Launched in 1900 at Connah's Quay, North Wales, she is typical of the sailing vessels which carried so much of the coastal trade up to the First World War, and had been the mainstay of the Newfoundland fish and Mediterranean fruit trades before that. The *Kathleen & May's* working life did not end until 1960 when she was one of the last four of the old sailing craft in service in Britain. In 1970 she was bought by the Maritime Trust in North Devon, made seaworthy at Bideford, brought round to Plymouth for restoration, and laid up in Sutton Harbour in 1972, where she attracted a constant stream of visitors.

But after a few years the Maritime Trust found that the single ship did not generate enough revenue, and moved her to St Katherine's Dock in the Pool of London to join the rest of their fleet.

CHAPTER 5
QUAYS AND RAILWAYS

A ridge of limestone runs from Mount Wise, on the banks of the Tamar, almost due east to Yealmpton and beyond. Its cliffs are the northern shore of Plymouth Sound and the Hoe still shows its natural shape. During the last Ice Age when the sea level was 200 ft below the present line and the south coast of Devon out by Eddystone, the river Plym cut a deep gorge through this limestone which, as the ice cap melted and the sea assumed its present level, became a deep channel. Between the Lambhay slopes on the eastern sides of the Hoe and the western cliffs of Cattedown there was another gap in the limestone through which the sea flowed. There is no strong river here to have carved a gap, but the little streams draining the slopes of North Hill probably filled up a natural basin in the softer slates and shillets behind the limestone, to form a pool which in time would have spilled over a low point in the limestone ridge and gradually cut it deeper.

When the sea came back that basin in the shillet became Sutton Pool, and the narrow cut it had worn through the limestone its mouth. Nature even furnished its own breakwater: a line of volcanic rock which ran through the limestone, parallel and close to its northern edge, offered more resistance to the sea than the limestone and became a ridge of rocks across the entrance. The present piers are built on those rocks.

The geological sketch on this page makes the formation clear. The scour of the sea would also have helped shape the pool into a near circle and then, as the town grew, its rubbish and the buildings of quays altered the shape to the present four-pointed star. Old streets still mark the original banks of Sutton Pool. If one starts on the West Pier and walks along the Barbican, up Southside Street to Notte Street then turns right into Woolster Street and continues by way of Vauxhall Street, Bretonside and Sutton Road to the head of Coxside Creek, one always has rising ground on the left hand and flat ground on the right. The flat land has all been recovered from the pool, the rising land is the old natural slope. Southside

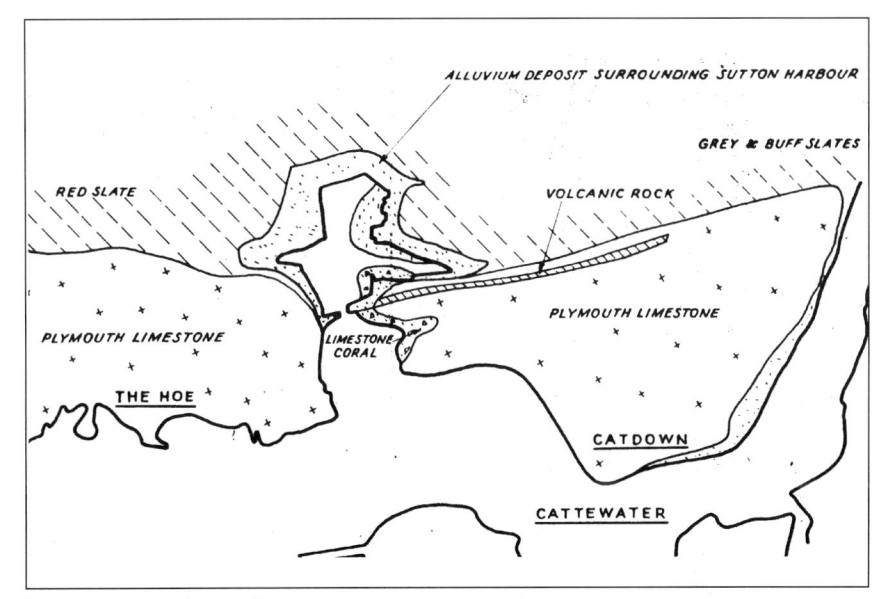

The geological structure of Sutton Harbour.

SUTTON HARBOUR

'A Plan of Sutton Pool with the adjacent keys and buildings, 1786'. This was a working plan used in the Duchy Office with later alterations up to 1822 marked in. East and West Piers can be seen drawn in over the Fish House, and a broken line marks the projected Sutton Wharf.

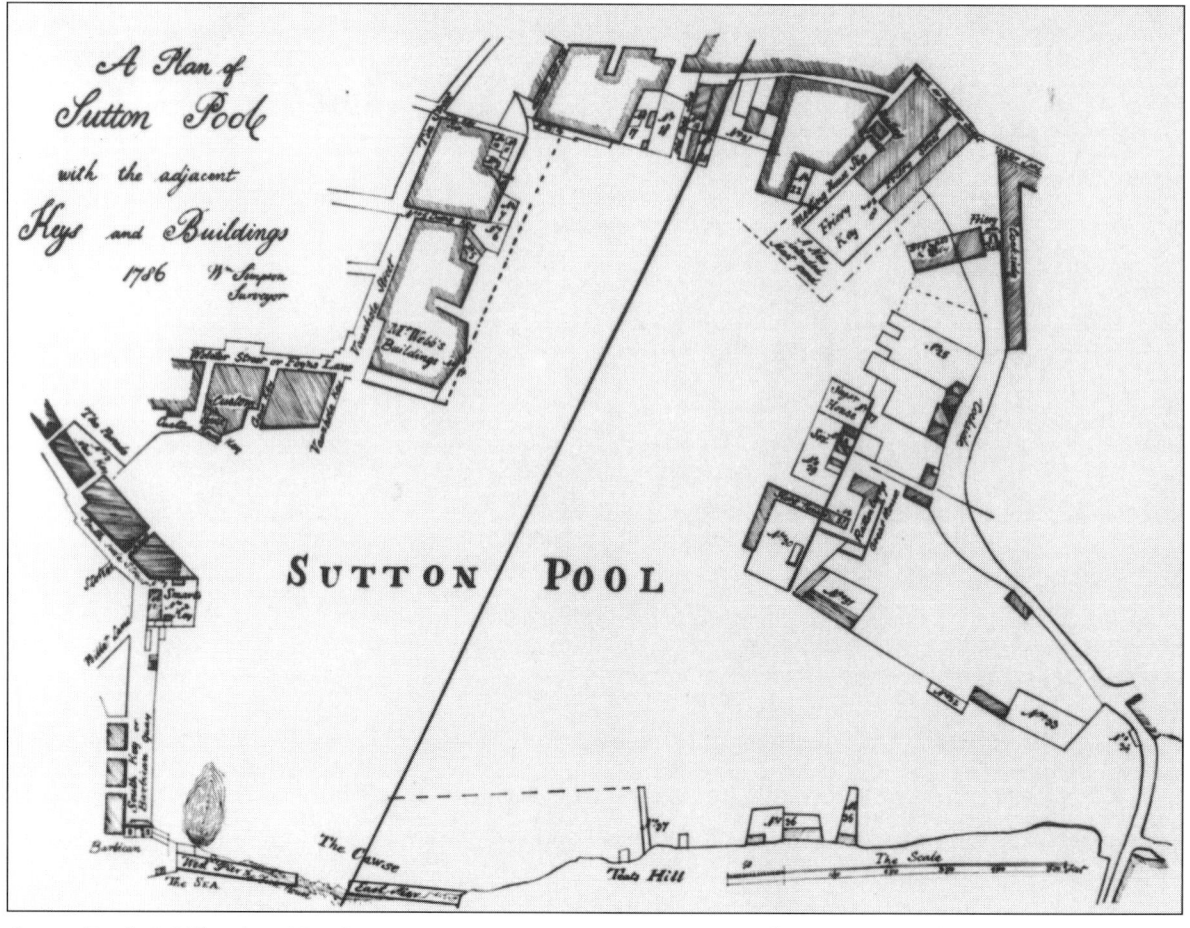

Street, Bayly's Wharf and Lockyer's Quay, are virtually in a straight line, and mark the northern edge of the limestone.

Centuries of tin streaming and china clay working on Dartmoor have silted the Plym estuary considerably, but the moorings between Cattedown and Turnchapel still have over 30 ft of water at low tide, and right up at Laira Bridge engineers had to sink their foundations through 60 feet of mud to find hard rock. Sutton Pool by comparison is very shallow and bores only go a few feet below the mud to reach the harder shillet and clays. The centre of the Pool, the deepest part, has about 8 ft of water at low water springs, with a bed about 3 ft thick of soft clay over harder shale and gravel.

Plymouth however, has a big tidal range, reaching up to 20 ft at maximum. Mean low water spring tides have nearly 2 ft of water over the chart figures, and mean high water neaps over 17 ft. It was this tidal range that made Sutton a workable harbour, for ships of 20 ft draught could be berthed at high tide, and sit without trouble on the soft mud at low tide.

The Fish Market in 1883, with the fish gutting, the buying and selling, all done on the Barbican cobbles, mixed up with people and dogs, horses and carts. An oil painting by W. Gibbons, dated 1883, in the board room of the Sutton Harbour Company.

An aerial view of Sutton Harbour in 1996 with the lock gates in operation, and the new Fish Market on the eastern side of the harbour in action. Even human access to the floor is limited, in the interests of hygiene. Photographed by Peter Holdgate, picture editor of the Evening Herald.

The China House (left), Britain's oldest waterside warehouse now converted into a public house and restaurant, which looks out on Sutton Harbour marina, with the fish market and the trawlers tied up alongside the quay in the background. Sutton Harbour.

A panoramic photograph of the south-eastern side of Sutton Harbour, stretching from the lock gates (right) and past the Fish Market to the top of Coxside Creek, with trawlers moored the full length of the quay. Sutton Harbour.

The sea walls for the quay extension being put into place, and the wide opening at the harbour entrance waiting for the final placing of the lock. Sutton Harbour.

The lock under construction at the top of the Coxside Creek before the decks were laid over the flotation chambers. Sutton Harbour.

Dawn on St George's Day, 23 April 1993, with Admiralty tugs manouevering the 9000 tons of concrete that made up the lock from the building site at the head of Coxside Creek into its final resting place at the harbour entrance.

The fish quay on a normal morning, with trawlers lining the sea wall after unloading for the market, and the various market firms, buyers, processors, packers and so forth, busy in their units (right). Sutton Harbour.

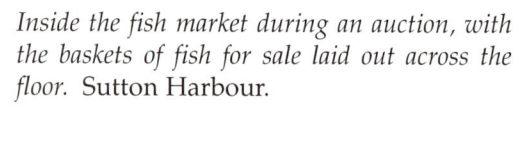

Inside the fish market during an auction, with the baskets of fish for sale laid out across the floor. Sutton Harbour.

(left) Peter Bromley, the Sutton Harbour's fisheries manager and (right) Shaun Lyth, Plymouth Trawler Agents' manager and auctioneer. Sutton Harbour.

From burly fisherman handling heavy maunds full of fish fresh from the sea, to shop assistants showing off delicate glassware; the 1890s fish market is now converted into a showroom for visitors. The glass is actually made in front of spectators and fired in the furnace (left) of Dartington Glass. Sutton Harbour.

A City Council contribution to the rehabilitation of the area; a symbol of fishing dominates the end of Mayflower Pier. Public art in this style has been used all around the perimeters of the Barbican area to attract and direct tourists. Sutton Harbour.

(Above) Sutton Harbour marina office at the end of the Sutton Jetty. Sutton Harbour.

The transformation of North Quay; where coal, fruit, salt and assorted cargoes came ashore. The warehouses have been replaced between 1986 and 1996 with flats, Harbourside Court, (left) and Mariner's Court (right), and an office block, North Quay House, between them. Sutton Harbour.

Farewell to the old fish market: a Lenkiewicz painting of a group of fisherman with the new market in the background. All are portraits of well-known characters; centre behind the tray of mackerel is Fred Brimacombe, doyen of the market; sitting extreme right is Dave Pessell, chairman of Plymouth Trawler Agents Ltd and standing extreme left is Duncan Godefroy, managing director of Sutton Harbour Co Ltd. The picture hangs in the Sutton Harbour Office. Sutton Harbour.

QUAYS AND RAILWAYS

There have been one or two cases of ships being damaged when grounding on uneven bottoms at low water over the years, but usually they were found in the law courts to have been old boats lacking the strength they should have had.

Before the piers were built the hard volcanic rocks reached out from Teat's Hill (Thomas Teate bought this land and established a ropewalk there before 1665). The part nearest the eastern shore was covered at high tide but the harbour entrance was close to the Barbican. The Mayflower Stone is on the edge of the old entrance; the 'Gut' as it was called. The tide must have poured in and out with some vigour, and just inside was a deep pool. Behind the rocks was the Cawse, or Cawsey, which has long been a puzzle. Its name is clearly causeway, and old town records show that stone was used to repair it. It has been thought of as a low stone jetty reaching out to the water's edge at low tide, but the 1786 survey of Sutton Harbour by William Simpson (shown opposite), suggests that it was a causeway right over to the eastern shore, which could probably be walked at low tide like the causeway between Newton Ferrers and Noss Mayo. It was there before 1486, when the earliest town accounts show it being repaired.

THE FISH HOUSE

On the rocks in the middle of the entrance was the Fish House, a very ancient stone structure with no windows on the seaward side, which served as a breakwater. Its age is unknown and its name is not explained, though it may have been used for storing fish, or even curing them (the smell would have been away from the town). In Queen Anne's reign it housed naval stores, and was finally washed away in a great storm in 1744. This probably led to the new piers at the entrance later in the century. The Fish House is clearly shown in the Gomme drawing of 1666 (see page 24), with a ship anchored in its lee. The defensive chain which was stretched across the Gut would have been secured to one corner of the Fish House, and brought up to a windlass or capstan on the stumpy little pier on the other side of the Gut, in front of the Barbican Gatehouse. There was also a mast with iron spikes in it, used as a boom.

Inside the harbour, grassy slopes ran down to the rocks at the water's edge, with muddy beaches in front at low tide, rather like Hooe Lake (which has the same geological history) at the present time. The town first reached the waterfront on the north bank of the Parade inlet, and excavations by James Barber revealed thirteenth and fourteenth century houses whose seaward walls were washed by the tide. These were at the foot of High Street, under the 1970 flats in Vauxhall Street, and were probably both the storehouses and homes of early merchants.

The flat area round the Parade is almost certainly the six acres of land recovered from the sea mentioned in the legal action of 1317 as belonging to the King, and the other royal property, five perches by one perch, was probably the first open quay built in the harbour. The legal award says it belonged to the King before the foundation of the ville of Sutton, which must mean before 1254, when Sutton was made a market town.

One can say that the north side of the Parade, out to Vauxhall Quay, was built up with warehouses and quays probably by 1400, and certainly by 1500. The defence map of Henry VIII, made about 1535, shows this with ships moored off Vauxhall Quay. Although the map has buildings facing Sutton Wharf, the shore in front looks to be in its natural state.

The revival of trade in Tudor times brought new quays: a Crane Quay, William Pull's Quay,

SUTTON HARBOUR

and Allyn's Quay are mentioned in 1519-20. There is no clue to their position now, but the logical place to look would be the south side of the Parade. Hawkins's Quay is named in 1558 as the sole quay in Plymouth at which goods could be landed. The Old Custom House on the Parade was repaired in 1586 so it is clearly much older; certainly the arches over the doors and windows resemble those in the Prysten House of St Andrew's, built 1490-1500. This building, the Ship Inn, and the warehouses out to the corner by the Navy Inn are all in one line; the tide washed the warehouse walls until 1891, and these are probably the 'quays' of the first half of the sixteenth century. The warehouses themselves have been so rebuilt and repaired over the centuries that it would be foolhardy to date them, but one, lower than the others, may well contain much original material.

The Barbican Quay, built before Hawkins in 1572, seen here in sailing trawler days, before the fish market was built in the 1890s.

BARBICAN BUILT

Dating becomes easier after this date. Plymouth's 'Black Book', its early record, has entered for 1572 'this yere the kaye on southesyde, whereof the southe ende adjoneth to the Barbygan vnderneath the Castell. Builded by the towne vnder full sea marcke, and Contayneth in lengethe one hundred and Thurtie Foot and in Bredethe fourtie and fower foot.' This was built when William Hawkins's privateering fleet was making the harbour so busy, and is the quay between the houses and the boundary stones that mark off the fish market extension. In 1584 there is a reference to 'newe kaies' which probably means an extension northwards of the Barbican quay. In 1584 the Barbican steps were made, and in 1602 'this yere also is the kaie made downe by John Smartes door.' Smart's Quay only disappeared when the fish market was built; Smart's house must have stood on the site of the present Navy Inn and the quay was a jetty about 50 ft square extending out into the harbour and making the corner into the Parade inlet. The head of the Parade already had the shape we know, apart from a cut shaped like a dock in front of the houses on the southern side. There was a legal argument in Lord Arundell's time as to whether the Parade, or New Quay, had or had not been built before 1576. At any rate by 1602 there was a continuous line of quays and warehouses from the Barbican pier to Vauxhall Quay.

There may have been more. A 1661 inquiry into the boundaries of Sutton Pool lists over two dozen quays, houses, cellars and palaces—both 'cellar' and 'palace' can be translated as warehouse or store; the palaces were not regal and the cellars were not underground; their names show them stretching right round the harbour. The Dung Quay was at the foot of Looe Street, the

QUAYS AND RAILWAYS

The morning after the great storm of November 1824, when the seaward side of Teat's Hill and right around Deadman's Bay was littered with wrecks. A sketch by Nicholas Condy. The same storm saw a ship sunk right inside Sutton Harbour, and another much damaged.

palace near the Great Tree was at the bottom of North Street, Friary Quay in the north-east corner, and buildings near Coxside and Teat's Quay must have stretched round the eastern shore. Coxside in early forms is Cock's side. Lucas Cock was Mayor in 1568 and Captain Cock, said to have lived at 51 Southside Street, was the only English captain killed in the battles against the Armada. Lucretia Cock owned harbourside property in 1754.

Some of these developments were certainly built in the Commonwealth but most probably they are all pre-Civil War, dating from the prosperous years of 1570-1640.

Probably therefore Sutton Harbour by 1640 had the outline, the ragged mixture of warehouses with little 'slips' between them running to the waterfront, and some small quays, that is shown in the eighteenth century maps. To visualise this one must mentally remove the wide straight wharfs that now enclose the northern part of the harbour, and see the water lapping the walls of the stores that back these wharfs. Some of the buildings behind Sutton Wharf, for instance, may be the originals of the seventeenth century, and Coxside waterfront probably has not changed much at all. One can still see there warehouses reaching out into the tide with water on three sides. The biggest open quay in the northern harbour was Friary Quay, about 50 ft square, projecting out into the harbour in front of Friary Street, and on the same line.

NEW MEN BUSY

Simpson's 1786 survey shows more or less the same outline. But all this tangled plan was to be changed in the nineteenth century to produce the wide quays enclosing three-quarters of the harbour as we know it today. Much of this development, like the Sutton Harbour Company itself, was to be shaped by railway developments and rivalries.

The first new quay directly sprang from the original Sutton Pool Company's formation in 1811. They started to build Sutton Wharf as soon as they were incorporated, spending £525 in 1813, £52 649 in 1814 and £28, obviously the finishing touch, in 1815. Their wharf ran north from the corner of Little Vauxhall Quay; previously this

51

SUTTON HARBOUR

Coxside Creek in the nineteenth century, with Shepherd's Wharf on the left and Lockyer's Quay on the right. Behind the figures on the quay is the limestone facade of the former prisoner of war barracks, the gateway of which has been rebuilt in front of the multi-storey car park.

waterfront had been a line of warehouses broken only by the Dung Quay, at the foot of Looe Street, and the Tin Quay at the foot of How Street. The Dung Quay, created in 1639, was what its name implied; all the street sweepings in the age of horses were collected there and the right to remove it auctioned annually. (see poster, page 15). It was shipped away as farm manure. Behind the Tin Quay, at the very north-west corner of the harbour was Tin Lane and the northern part of Vauxhall Street was known as Tin Street; from this corner no doubt the tin from Dartmoor was shipped.

The first Sutton Wharf may only have been half its present width, because much money was spent on it again in the 1830s. After the trade spurt of the late 1820s, J. M. Rendell (the engineer who built Laira Bridge and Embankments) was employed to plan new wharfs for Sutton, and he proposed wide quays all round the northern and eastern sides of the harbour. Little Vauxhall Quay dates from this time. The original narrow quay was built up with warehouses in 1822 by Edmund Lockyer and the present quay must have been built in front of these warehouses in the 1830s.

There was also development at the head of Coxside Creek. Thomas Tyrwhitt, now Sir Thomas, launched a plan in 1819 to build a horse-drawn railway from Princetown to Plymouth. Edmund Lockyer and William Elford joined him, the line was opened in 1823 and by December 1825 an extension to the head of Coxside Creek was completed. This was important for the Johnsons, quarry owners who, by paying for its construction, won control of the whole railway. They had among other contracts one to supply the granite to surface Plymouth Breakwater, then being built. The wharf at the head of Coxside Creek is still called Johnson's Quay, and alongside it, running half the length of the south side of the creek, is Lockyer's Quay, named after the railway partner who had a finger in so many Plymouth pies at that time. It dates from 1833. One of the yards Lockyer owned behind the quay had a spur of the railway entering it, and is labelled 'copper ore yard' on a contemporary plan. The ore must have come down by the Plympton branch of the railway, opened in 1834, from the Bottle Hill mines near Plympton.

RAILWAYS ARRIVE

In the railway battles of the 1840s, Brunel's wharf plan for Sutton largely followed those of Rendell. His railway plan visualized an entirely new line into Sutton, independent of the Dartmoor route and reaching the north-east corner of the harbour. When the high hopes for Sutton evaporated and the Great Western moved its interest to Millbay, they still had Parliamentary power for a line to

Sutton. The main line crossed the Dartmoor railway at Marsh Mills, so they bought the Dartmoor line from there in, and alongside the Dartmoor's 4 ft 6 in gauge laid in a third rail to provide their broad gauge of 7 ft 0 1/4 in. This was completed by May 1853 and the wooden hut which had served for passengers on the arrival platform at Laira, Plymouth's first railway station, was rebuilt as a goods shed at what was now distinguished as Sutton Harbour Railway Station.

It was a mix-up of a railway, with horse-drawn traffic bringing Dartmoor granite and, after 1853, china clay from Lee Moor. So the GWR used horses to draw their trucks as well and not until 1869, when the GWR shook off the local horse traffic, did they remove the 4 ft 6 in rail and make the line broad gauge only, with locomotives drawing the trucks. The age of steam on land had at last reached Sutton Harbour.

This was slow development after the high hopes of 1844. The Sutton Harbour Improvement Company Act of 1847, which had brought in the London and South-Western Railway after the GWR defection, gave the new company power to build quays and railways. Within three months of the Act becoming law they deposited plans to build North Quay. Joseph Locke was the engineer. Until then there was a short and narrow wharf at the cooperage end and then a continuous line of stores right to the water's edge, only broken by the end of Old Tree Slip, now called Hawker's Avenue. The new North Quay, built in 1849-50, reached from the end of Sutton Wharf to Moore's slipway, in the north-east corner of the harbour.

But the decade after the GWR steam locomotives reached Coxside in 1869 produced tremendous changes. The L&SWR was in striking distance of Plymouth, and this spurred the GWR to new activity. Both were wooing the Sutton Harbour traffic, and so the Improvement Company was busy too. The Harbour Company in 1871 deposited plans by W. R. Galbraith for a tramway to encircle the whole harbour. The approach was to be across Exeter Street, with one spur going along Sutton Road to the station at Coxside. The other spur was to go along North Quay, with a turntable at the end to make the right-angle turn on to Sutton Wharf, another turntable at the end to take the line on to Vauxhall Quay, yet another turntable at the end to reach Little Vauxhall Quay, and then a viaduct across the Parade inlet to carry the lines on to the Barbican and a terminus at the foot of the Western Pier.

In February 1872 the half-yearly meeting of the Company was told that the GWR was projecting an extension of their line from Laira to North Quay, with a station on Sutton Road. The L&SWR had won running power over the GWR's Launceston line from Lydford down, which would bring them at long last into Plymouth, and they were proposing to build a new and independent narrow gauge line from Laira to North Quay, with a station at Friary Gardens. Here was

Sutton Wharf at the corner of North Quay, painted in 1886 by William Pearn. The Sutton Harbour Inn is long forgotten.

SUTTON HARBOUR

progress; the prospect of railway lines all round the Pool from West Pier to Coxside, linked with two main line systems and both narrow and broad gauge. The Sutton Harbour directors once more revived hopes of an enclosed dock, and launced a Bill in Parliament.

IN-FIGHTING

A period of intensive railway in-fighting ensued, with the various rights to Sutton Harbour being used by both parties as bargaining cards. In 1873 the L&SWR, in whom Sutton Harbour had pinned its hopes after the GWR abandoned them in 1846, not only abandoned their fight to take their line past the projected Friary Station, but as part of the deal got a branch line to the west shore of Stonehouse Pool. This new idea was to develop Ocean Quay, where liners could come alongside, and so capture the now-thriving ocean mail traffic which the GWR was handling through tenders from Millbay. The Stonehouse project was in time completed but never really dented the Millbay traffic; what it really did was to kill off

A 1938 aerial view of the northern end of the harbour showing clearly the railway lines around this end of the harbour. Probably all the waterfront in this picture was like the stretch between the China House and North-East Quay, before the straight quays were built.

QUAYS AND RAILWAYS

the last hope Sutton had of becoming a wet dock, a project only feasible with railway money. Sutton Harbour in 1874 finally had Parliamentary approval for its dock, but not the financial backing. Ironically enough the Duchy had increased the rent in anticipation of bigger profits, so the Harbour Company was really worse off. But in 1873 the GWR did build their second line into the harbour, swinging off from the old Dartmoor route at the point where it passed under Cattedown Road, and passing along the back of St John's Road to reach a new station on Sutton Road.

In 1878 the L&SWR opened Friary as a goods station, and one line in the marshalling yard behind the station finished just short of Exeter Street. At a cost of £25 000 the Harbour Company was busy building the North-East Quay, which cut through the clutter of old shipyards, quays, and storehouses there, and cleared the path for both railways to reach North Quay in 1879, the L&SWR on 22 October and the GWR on 6 November. The GWR had to take a spur off their new line to Coxside Station at St John's Bridge to get the line of approach. They were still broad guage and the L&SWR standard gauge, so there had to be three rails to each track once they joined up on North Quay. This hybrid was carried to Sutton Wharf and Vauxhall Quay, turning the corners by turntable as proposed earlier but never making the viaduct leap across to the Barbican. Only three years later the GWR switched over from broad to standard gauge and the third rail was taken up in Sutton Harbour. On Sutton Wharf the line of cobbles mark the old broad rail, and at a set of points in front of the door into Dolphin House is the last piece of broad gauge line in the country in its original position.

Sutton Harbour's railway history is full of puzzles, and the maze of four lines crossing Sutton Road, together with the light railways to serve particular warehouses would have been an industrial archaeologist's dream of heaven. The tunnel under Exeter Street to Friary is trackless and overgrown. Most of the original railway lines still encircle the northern harbour, but ceased to be used after the Second World War. One odd survival of the pre-motor age remains, the archway of the horsewash, a tunnel from the east side of Harbour Avenue under North East Quay to the tide line. Before all these quays were built several of the slipways ended in beaches where the carters since time out of mind had washed their horses. The company did not forget them.

The L&SWR, which got to Sutton thirty-three years too late to fight the GWR, was in 1879-80 building another line to the Cattedown water-

In this aerial view two colliers are unloading at Bayly's Wharf opposite the timber yard where wood lies seasoning in a pond. The GWR system can be seen on the right.

55

front, extending it in 1882, and building another line round to Turnchapel on the other side of Cattewater in 1897. From these lines sprang the rapid trade growth of Cattewater. Poor Sutton; all the railways had done for her was to create rivals at Cattewater, Millbay and even Stonehouse.

But the company was still busy improving the harbour. By 1893 Sutton Jetty, complete with rails, extended Sutton Wharf southwards on wooden piles. With the rapidly increasing growth in the town the silting problem was severe. There were two sewers with outfalls off Fisher's Nose and Deadman's Bay but many of the town drains emptied straight into the harbour. John Pethick the contractor was employed and he dredged 33 000 tons from the harbour bed in 1882. Even then it was estimated that there were still 27 500 tons of sewage on the harbour bottom. Demands that the Corporation should pay for this met violent opposition, and 'one gentleman who took an active part in the affairs of the town' was quoted as saying that they should expect no assistance; the harbour was the natural cesspool of the town and they should accept it in its natural condition. It was at this time that the increasing fish trade was causing such congestion on the Barbican and the Corporation was toying with the idea of building a new fish market itself.

NEW PLAN

Led by Tom Pitts as chairman, Robert Bayly as vice-chairman and William Luscombe, lone survivor of the 1847 founders, the Improvement Company in November 1888 published its plans to solve both problems at one stroke. They proposed widening the Barbican from West Pier to the present White House Pier, and building Quay Road in front of the warehouses to link up with the Parade. It provided wharfage of 1048 ft in place of the previous 370 ft, and Quay Road also relieved traffic pressure on Southside Street. In addition a new fish market was to be sited on the extension, leaving the old Barbican clear as a highway. The Barbican extension was to cover huge tanks into which would be piped all the sewage that had previously gone into the harbour, and from there dispersed in the sea through the Fisher's Nose outfall. This development needed an Act of Parliament.

The Bill was fought by the GWR, who were plainly just trading rivals, and Plymouth Corporation. This latter caused strong local feeling; there were even suggestions of rigged votes in the Council. The Bill became law, with various compromises, but the Corporation managed to push the poor law rates on the harbour up from £310 a year to over £500.

The railway tangle went on. J. C. Inglis, who in 1892 became engineer-in-chief to the GWR and later Sir John, had prepared the plans for the fish market extension which his company then opposed in Parliament. He continued to supervise the actual work in Sutton Harbour after his promotion but at the same time the GWR was giving preferential railway rates to Millbay Docks as against traffic coming from the other harbours in Plymouth. The L&SWR was paying the Improvement Company £1000 a year for the exclusive rights to the lines round the harbour (which were owned by the company) but at the same time the L&SWR was improving Stonehouse, the quays were growing at Cattedown because of their line, and the L&SWR had finally pinned its colours to the Southampton mast by buying the docks there in 1892.

But the Improvement Company went ahead. By April 1892 another 20 000 tons of silt had been dredged, and rocks were removed from between

QUAYS AND RAILWAYS

the pierheads to give seven feet of water at the lowest tides. The fish market extension was not completed on time (uneven bricks used in the sewage tanks meant a partial rebuilding) and another Act of Parliament had to be obtained in 1895 to extend the time limit. The new Act also included authority to extend Lockyer's Quay at Coxside. While this was being built the Corporation came up with a plan to take over the Cattewater, extend Batten Breakwater (built in 1883), and develop an extensive complex of docks, quays, and warehouses from Queen Anne's Battery to Victoria Wharf with supporting roads and railways, and deepen the Cattewater right up to Laira Bridge. The Admiralty vetoed this with a collection of demands impossible to meet.

The new quay at Coxside, named Bayly's Wharf after the then chairman of the Improvement Company, was opened on 12 May 1900 by the steamer *Newark* which came in with 1500 tons of coal for the Gas Company. The latest steam cranes were set up on the wharf, and it soon became the focal point for all the harbour's domestic coal trade, most of which had previously been on North Quay. New warehouses were being built at the same time on the North-East Quay. Apart from the rebuilding of certain warehouses, notably the Co-op premises on North Quay, more modern gantries on Bayly's Wharf, the infilling of gaps left by the bombs of 1941, and the 1969 Fish Quay modernizations, Sutton Harbour did not materially change its appearance until 1972.

MARINA STARTS

Seventy pontoon moorings for yachts were laid down off Sutton Wharf. Within two weeks of their opening all the berths were taken. The number was increased to 150 in 1973 and 200 in 1974; they were all taken at once and by 1975 another 200 yachts were on a waiting list. Every boat owner has a car parking space, the pontoons are floodlit at night, and are all equipped with water, fire extinguishers, life-lines and life-belts. By the end of 1974 an amenity block had been built at the angle of Sutton Wharf and North Quay with lavatories and showers on the ground floor and a control office for the berthing masters above. In their office also is a VHF radio transmitter and receiver through which yachts at sea can make contact. It also provides a valuable service to fishing vessels at sea who can telephone their estimated time of arrival and size of catch. In 1974 a pollution control craft was bought by Sutton Harbour to help keep the Pool clean; it can also carry out maintenance dredging and has fire-fighting equipment.

The first arrangment of the pontoons for the marina. Note the conveyor gantry crossing Sutton Quay to what is now Dolphin Court. Sutton Jetty behind was entirely taken up by the sea angling club and over the entrance a sign proclaims 'Barbican Angling Marina'.

CHAPTER 6
COLONISATION

On 9 April 1585 seven little ships sailed out of Sutton Harbour, the *Tiger, Roebuck, Lion, Elizabeth, Dorothy*, and two small pinnaces, with Sir Richard Grenville as admiral. On 17 August a colony of 107 men, with Ralph Lane in command and Philip Amadas, a Plymouth man, as his deputy, was set up on Roanoke Island, in what is now North Carolina. It was England's first colony in the New World.

Plymouth seamen and merchants had opened up America to our ships but it was the gentlemen of Devon, with university education, experience of plantations in Ireland, and large capital resources in their land-holdings, who realized that the true future lay in settlement. The Gilberts of Dartmouth had been early in the field; but this 1585 expedition in which Grenville's cousin, Walter Ralegh, was the moving spirit, was the first actual plantation.

Before Grenville could get back with more supplies in the next summer, Drake had called on the colony, and acceded to their request to bring them home. Grenville arrived a fortnight later; he left a new company of fifteen men. On 8 May 1587 a second major colonizing party sailed out of Sutton Pool in three ships, but at Roanoke they only found the bones of one of the fifteen men they expected to see. Nothing daunted the new party, ninety-one men, seventeen women and nine children, moved ashore. Next year the Armada sailed, stopping the relief ships, and then the *Hopewell*, the *John Evangelist* and the *Little John* did leave Plymouth with supplies; it was 20 March 1590. They found Roanoke deserted, with just the name of another island, Croatoan, carved on a gatepost. Storms stopped them going to Croatoan, but there was no trace found of this second colony. The search continued, on and off, for thirteen years; the only report obtained of the missing men, women and children was that they had been 'adopted' by an Indian tribe. Modern research has established that they did move a few miles to the north where they were 'adopted' by an Indian tribe and in two or three generations of cross-breeding the white skins and English memories had been lost in the Indian culture.

But exploration continued on the American coast and in 1605 Captain George Weymouth brought back five Indians from what we now call New England. Three he gave to Sir Ferdinando Gorges, captain of Plymouth Fort. The next year King James I granted two charters for colonization in America, one to a group of London merchants whose spheres of influence was south of what is now New York, and the other to Plymouth merchants, led by Gorges, whose writ ran on the coast to the north. Both companies planted colonies in 1607. The London colony, at Jamestown, survived. The Plymouth men, at the mouth of the Kennebec in modern Maine, with two of Gorge's Indians as guides, came through the winter but one leader died and the other,

Ralegh Gilbert, was told next spring by the relief ships that his brother had died and he must come home to administer the family estates. Rather than stay leaderless, the whole party returned.

But Plymouth became the supply base for Jamestown. The biggest relief fleet sailed out in 1609 and one of the commanders, Sir George Somers, was wrecked on Bermuda and he wintered there. From this sprang the colonisation of the island. Captain John Smith, one of the great leaders of the Jamestown venture, was often in Plymouth trying to persuade the merchants there to renew their colonizing efforts, but they were doing well enough fishing on the New England coast in the summer months, and trading with the Indians for furs. Smith made a map of New England (he invented the term) which he took to the Prince of Wales, later Charles I, to give names to the prominent features, and Prince Charles wrote 'Plymouth' against one of the summer trading posts, opposite Cape Cod. One of the arrivals in old Plymouth in 1616 was Pocohontas, the Indian princess who years before had pleaded for John Smith's life when he was captured by her father in Virginia. Now she was married and accompanied by her tobacco-planter husband, John Rolfe; she was to die at Gravesend when taking ship for the return voyage. Another Indian who came into Sutton Pool at about this time was sent by Pocohontas's father with instructions to count the English. He came ashore with a large stick and a knife, to make a notch for every man he saw. He soon gave up.

THE MAYFLOWER

In August 1620 two ships came into Sutton Harbour with a strange company. Most of them were advanced Puritans, Separatists who had left the Church of England, and England, to worship in their own way, and had been settled in Holland for a dozen years. With them were people, mainly like-minded in religion, from Southwark and Essex. They had a charter to set up a colony in the northern part of the London Company of Virginia's land, somewhere near the mouth of the Hudson River. This was the sort of project that Plymouth people knew all about, but it was too late in the season to be crossing the Atlantic—the eight Plymouth ships fishing off New England that summer and the forty or fifty on the Newfoundland banks, were about to sail home before the onset of winter.

The master of the biggest ship, the *Mayflower*, Christopher Jones from Rotherhithe, seemed only to have 'home trade' experience from the Baltic to the Bay of Biscay. His first mate had been to Jamestown and his second mate had once been on the New England coast, and one of the prospective colonists had been in Virginia, but they must have seemed strangely lacking in experience for such a venture. Captain John Smith himself may

The sea wall of West Pier supports a row of plaques commemorating the great voyages of colonisation that have started from Plymouth. By the end of the 1980s there were so many plaques that they were overflowing on to the wall on the opposite side of the road.

SUTTON HARBOUR

Large crowds watched the 300th Mayflower anniversary celebrations in Plymouth in 1920. Here the 'Pilgrims' process from the Barbican up to the Hoe for a 'farewell service'.

have been in Plymouth; certainly at some time in 1620 he was trying to persuade these people to make him their captain. They had instead engaged a captain from the north of England, Miles Standish, whose military experience had been in the Low Countries.

They seemed to have little money, and were not too well stocked with stores. Before they left Southampton, where the two groups had met together, they had had to sell most of their butter to pay their bills. The second ship, the *Speedwell*, was giving trouble. They had put into Dartmouth for *Speedwell* to be examined, and they had come into Plymouth for the same reason, though nothing could be found wrong with the ship. Probably in rerigging her for the ocean crossing she had been given too heavy spars and possibly over-canvassed, for in a seaway she seemed to work and open up. The people who had been in *Speedwell* had been dreadfully sick and many feared for the safety of their families - for wives and children were in this company.

There would have been much sympathy in Plymouth for this group of people. Most of the men were away, either across the Atlantic or out with Sir Robert Mansell and Sir Richard Hawkins in an expedition that had sailed from Plymouth a month earlier to burn out the pirates of Algiers. But the old men, and the women in the port, knew all about the Atlantic and the problems of life in America. They were Puritans as well, with a strong Puritan vicar at St Andrew's and a renowned Puritan pamphleteer as the lecturer there. So they looked after these people facing such a deperate venture, and quite likely had some of these as guests in their houses while the decision was reached to pay off *Speedwell* and go on, those who were still willing and for whom there was room, in *Mayflower* alone. They stood on the New Quay and on the Barbican pier on 6 September 1620 to watch them sail off with a good strong north-east wind behind them, and no doubt their prayers went with them.

Not for another year, when the New England fishing fleet came back in the autumn of 1621, would Plymouth have heard that these ill-assorted voyagers had made the crossing, had finally settled beside the harbour that John Smith had called Plymouth, and in spite of losing half their number in the first winter had built a village, and planted crops, and looked like surviving. Gorges had got a new patent for the Plymouth Company and revived it with new capital, and in 1623 David Thompson of Plymouth, with his wife Amyas and their four children, had crossed with the fishermen and set up home in New England, the first neighbour of the people at the new Plymouth. Years later the historian of the Pilgrims, for so those *Mayflower* passengers came to be called, said that they kept the name for their new town because it was the last town they saw in their native country, and because 'they received many kindnesses from some Christians there.'

SETTLERS FROM PLYMOUTH

In the decade after the Pilgrims a number of Plymouth men moved over the ocean, founding scattered settlements. In 1630 the troubles between King Charles and his Puritan subjects led to a big exodus in which, of the 1000 people who went, about 150 from the western counties sailed from Plymouth. They had 'a day of solemn prayer and fasting' in the new Hospital of Poor's Portion, in Catherine Street, before they sailed. The Hospital, which had been built by the Puritan merchants and ship-owners of Plymouth to care for the old and sick, was pulled down in 1870 when the present Guildhall was built, but its entrance was preserved and has now been re-erected in the Elizabethan gardens behind New Street. The inscription in the lintel, 'By God's helpe through Christ,' can just be made out in the time-worn granite, and it is fitting that it should find a home within a stone's throw of the quay from which sailed these people who founded first Dorchester, now part of Boston, Mass., and a few years later the town of Windsor, Connecticut.

Right up to the outbreak of the Civil War the Plymouth ships fishing off New England were the main links of these colonists with England, and many more Plymouth people moved across the Atlantic. After the Civil War there was still the link of normal trading from Sutton Pool.

The explorations of the eighteenth century which opened up the Pacific and finally Australia and New Zealand were naval affairs. Through Byron in the *Dolphin* and *Tamar* in 1764, Wallis in the *Dolphin* in 1766, with Carteret in the *Swallow*, and all three of Cook's expeditions sailed from Plymouth, the new Dockyard would have been their base. But all of them would have been provisioned from the depot at Lambhay, and it is quite possible that Captain Cook brought the *Endeavour* in 1768, and the *Resolution* in 1772, and again in 1776, to anchor off the mouth of the Pool so that boats could ferry out the stores.

Two Plymouth men were closely connected with these voyages of exploration. Tobias Furneaux, from Swilly, was Wallis's second lieutenant and captain of the *Adventure* which accompanied Cook on his second voyage, during which he made the first chart of the south and east coast of Tasmania. William Bligh, son of a Cornishman, was born in Plymouth on 9 September 1754 and was only twenty-three when chosen to go with Cook on his third voyage, as a chart-maker. Tragically, it was his firing on fleeing natives that let to Captain Cook being killed in Hawaii. It was his voyage as captain of the *Bounty* to fetch breadfruit from Tahaiti to the West Indies that made him notorious, however, accused of the cruelty which led to the mutiny. But he should be remembered also as the splendid seaman who, when set adrift, made a 4000 miles voyage in an open boat to bring his companions to safety. Nelson praised him for his valour at the Battle of Copenhagen but Bligh was always in trouble; when he was sent to New South Wales as governor in 1805 he was deposed by another mutiny.

NEW PLYMOUTH

These men opened up the Pacific, and by 1839 Edward Gibbon Wakefield had formed the New Zealand Company intent on settling a colony there. Wakefield sailed with the first colonists in the *Tory*, embarking from the West Pier of Sutton Harbour on 12 May 1839. This so moved the mer-

The board on the side of Island House carries the names of all who sailed on the Mayflower.

The entrance to the Hospital of the Poor's Portion originally stood in Catherine Street. It has links with the founders of Dorchester, Massachusetts, USA.

SUTTON HARBOUR

chants of Plymouth that on 25 January 1840 the Plymouth Company of New Zealand was formed, with the Earl of Devon as governor, Thomas Gill deputy governor, and Thomas Woollcombe managing director. They bought 60 000 acres from the New Zealand Company, and their first party of settlers, 64 adults and 70 children, sailed from Sutton Harbour in the *William Bryan* on 19 November 1840. New Plymouth was founded on North Island, and in all the Plymouth New Zealand Company sent out six ships with 897 emigrants to the settlement, nearly all from Plymouth, Devon and Cornwall. But though this company was short-lived because of the failure of their London bankers and was merged into the main New Zealand Company, Plymouth was established in the emigration business.

EMIGRATION DEPOT

An 1845 plan of Sutton Harbour shows Elphinstone and Baltic wharfs, the old Lambhay Victualling Yard (by then replaced by the Royal William Yard at Stonehouse), as still owned by the Ordnance Board but in the occupation of Thomas Gill. In 1847 the storehouses at Elphinstone Wharf, between Phoenix Wharf and Fisher's Nose, were made into a Government Emigration Depot. Perhaps the choice of Plymouth owed something to the appointment of that time of Frederic Rogers, later Lord Blachford, as Assistant Under-Secretary for the Colonies and Commissioner for Emigration. There was already a steady flow from England to the United States and Canada; the end of transportation of convicts to Australia in 1840 made that a desirable place for settlement; New Zealand and the Cape of Good Hope were all developing. The arrival of the railway made Plymouth a more accessible port, and the Irish potato famine of 1847 launched a great move out of that country. A letter from Frederic Rogers gives a vivid picture of what was happening:

Plymouth, May 31, 1848

Our Irish workhouse girls arrived here by Monday's steamer from Dublin. I got to the Depot just in time to see the lighter (or barge) arrive full of them - a very pretty sight it was, one of those picturesque barges with dark red sails full of 185 bright cloaks and shawls of different colours, clean and new, and they came out picturesque but not pretty. In fact they are generally ugly and clumsy, though healthy and strong... The Presbyterians from Belfast are in grey ill-made gowns and tippets... The Wesleyan matron I hope will do well when on board. Meanwhile she has been blundering about her luggage. It has not arrived, and in an hour or two the ship will be ready to start except for her. Luckily the wind in contrary (it has just become so), else we should have the Earl Grey *with its three masts, captain, crew, and 200 emigrants, all waiting in port (perhaps losing the wind) for Mrs. C.'s portmanteau.*

Steamships were already running a regular service from Dublin and Cork to Plymouth. A deck passage from Cork to Plymouth cost half a guinea, and passages to North America could be had for eight guineas and to Australia for fourteen guineas. As the Australian states were given control of migration they offered assisted passages and grants of land. The finding of gold in California in 1848, and in Australia in 1851, produced a new impetus.

In 1847, 26 vessels sailed from Plymouth with 1730 emigrants; in 1848, 89 ships with 8505; and in 1849, 130 with 15 895 people. Of the 1849 ships, 109 cleared for Australia with 14 118 people, and

COLONISATION

10 for Canada with 1171. In 1856, 54 vessels sailed, with 8898 emigrants, 7000 for Australia and nearly all the rest for Canada. The main flow to the United States was concentrated through Liverpool; right through its fifty years in the business Plymouth's main concern was with Australia, New Zealand, the Cape, and Canada.

The Canadian business had started up as a result of the timber of the Baltic, essential to the English shipbuilding yards, being denied them in 1807. The Canadian forests were the obvious alternatives; it was even more economic to build ships in Canada and sail them home. As early as 1817 the Pope family, who were tenants of the Earl of Morley's shipyard at Turnchapel, had run out of work building warships with the end of the war. They sent two members of the family to Prince Edward Island. With farming depressed in Devon and Cornwall and, after the turn of the century, distress in the mining areas, there was every incentive to move out and these little ships which brought home timber returned with emigrants. In 1829 the ships of Chanter of Appledore were offering Atlantic passages from Plymouth at £3, or £25 for cabin passengers.

There was a scandal in 1855 when the barque *John* was wrecked almost as soon as she had left Sutton Harbour, and the master and crew left the 263 passengers to their fate. Most of them were from North Devon, and nearly all perished, yet only two years later it is recorded that some 200 people left North Devon in one week alone, to emigrate from Plymouth.

Against the Canadian emigration, in small ships, the Australian business was carried in large sailing craft which returned with wool and corn. Apart from these ships which made Plymouth their major point of departure, big clippers like

The Emigration Depot can be seen in this picture fronting the wharf beneath the Citadel ramparts. To the right of Phoenix Wharf is the biscuit factory. The Victualling Office stores on Commercial Wharf had already been demolished to allow for the road widening and linking with Madeira Road under the Hoe. The photograph was taken just before demolition in February 1937.

SUTTON HARBOUR

The Emigrant's Penny Magazine, to serve the constantly-changing population of the Emigration Depot, was published by the charitably-minded of Plymouth and ran for some years.

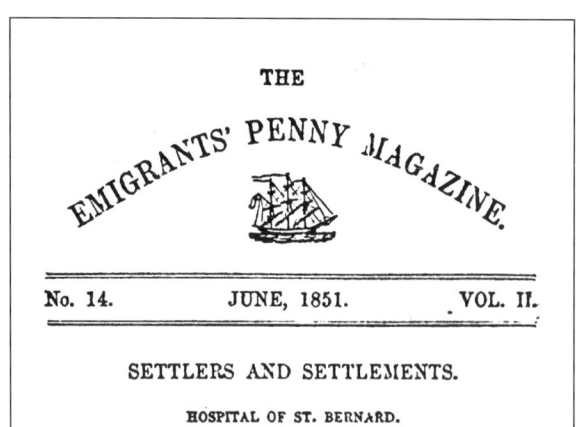

THE EMIGRANTS' PENNY MAGAZINE.

No. 14.   JUNE, 1851.   VOL. II.

SETTLERS AND SETTLEMENTS.

HOSPITAL OF ST. BERNARD.

(Concluded from page 84.)

On leaving the high road, which passes through the valley of the Rhone, in order to ascend the Great St. Bernard, the traveller winds through a valley in the centre of which rushes the river Drantz, forcing its impetuous way over its rocky bed, and forming a fine feature in the imposing landscape. For nearly fifteen English miles the road is embowered in fruit and forest trees, and enlivened by the bright verdure and innumerable flowers which are so conspicuous in Swiss scenery; but after leaving St. Pierre, a village about half way up the mountain, the country becomes more rugged, and the sublime preponderates over the beautiful. High rocks, whose rugged sides are washed by the mountain torrent, and fringed by the dark pine forest, form the nearer objects of view, whilst

those of the famous Black Ball line called for passengers, and small numbers embarked for the Cape of Good Hope, Port Natal, the eastern United States and San Francisco. White's *Directory* for 1850, describing Plymouth as 'celebrated as a port for emigration', whence over 25 000 had sailed in three years, said 'here are several respectable government and general emigration agents, and the vessels are generally of the best description, lying in Cattewater or the Sound...'

The Emigration Depot at Elphinstone housed the poor, those driven from Ireland or the western counties by poverty and depression, who were being given assisted passages. The Government Emigration Agent in 1852 was Lieut Carew, RN, and he told a health inquiry that the depot, capable of holding 500 emigrants, was supported by the Colonial Land Funds in Australia. Only those with an emigration order were admitted, and a vast number came from Ireland. It was in a healthy part of the town, was spacious, well-ventilated, and had no cesspools. There had been no deaths in the cholera outbreak of a year or two earlier, and in his five years there only twenty-five people had died, and those from wounds or infections caught in journeying to the depot. Those who arrived sick were placed in isolation, and in his view there would have been more disease, and much distress, without the depot in which the people could await their ships. The ladies of the town, he reported, gave time and money to help the people. He made no contrast but one cannot escape comparing the situation in Liverpool where the waiting people were at the mercy of every lodging-house keeper and bloodsucker in the port.

One can see how the poor made up the mass of emigrants from the figures; in 1859 for instance there were 338 cabin class emigrants as against 3,786 going steerage. Most that year are shown going to the 'East Indies', with New South Wales, Victoria, and the Cape of Good Hope also taking over 500 people each. Health conditions at the depot were falling, however, probably due to people coming from homes already long hit by poverty and their resistance to disease weakened by malnutrition. A report to Plymouth Public Dispensary in January 1860 showed that of 102 children who had died of measles in the town, 32 had been taken from the Emigration Depot. In October and November 47 people had died there, out of a total of 412 souls, a death rate of 114 per thousand compared with 6.38 for all Plymouth and a heavier mortality even than that of King Street West, a large and densely-crowded district.

But the flow went on. In 1876 over 10 000 people sailed in 25 ships, and in 1878 there were 15 500 in 100 ships, with a record exodus of 1800 in a week. At that time, apart from a civilian Government emigration officer whose job under the current legislation was to see that the ships and the rations were adequate, there were agents for New South Wales, South Australia, and New Zealand. The contractor, who ran the depot, was Arthur Hill of Reading. In 1883 he completed a scheme of improvements and extensions (even adding separate lavatories) which gave 1118 fixed berths, 372 for single men, 402 for single women, and 344 for married couples and children. There were five large mess rooms, and it was described as 'the only establishment of its kind on any considerable extent in the country.'

But the business was coming to an end. The United States had started a half-hearted check to immigration in 1882, but financial crises in both America and Australia in 1893 brought real checks, and a virtual end of the assisted passage schemes. The main exodus from Plymouth, at any rate, ended with the century, and so did the Elphinstone depot. Total figures of departure from Plymouth are only available for eight separate years, but they total nearly 70 000. One might hazard a guess that nearly all the quarter million assisted passages to Australia went from Plymouth, and that in all probably half a million English and Irish emigrants to the British colonies in the last century sailed from Sutton Pool.

Above: *a replica of the Nonsuch, the first ship of the Hudson Bay Company, in Sutton Harbour.*

Opposite: *The Mayflower Stone was originally set in the middle of West Pier on the exact spot (according to historian R.N. Worth) from which the Pilgrims would have embarked.*

CHAPTER 7
HOUSES, CHURCHES AND PUBS

Without the men and women who live and work round Sutton Pool, and the children whose rich playground stretches from the slopes of the Hoe down the cobbled alleys to the minute beaches unfolded at low tide, the harbour would be nothing. It is a creation of human activity, and there must be some brief record of how and where they have lived over the centuries.

The town the Plantagenet kings saw was closely confined to the small area between St Andrew's Church and the harbour. It could be bounded by a line from North Quay along Martin Lane to Bretonside, across the bus station to the top of New George Street, thence to St Andrew's tower, down Catherine Street to Notte Street, and thence to the inshore corner of the Parade. The main street, the High Street (now foolishly called Buckwell Street), at the top met the true Buckwell Street and Whimple Street, and in the triangle was an open-air market round a market cross. The first town hall, or Guildhall, was built there, probably like the surviving market halls of so many old English towns, a room on pillars whose open ground floor made a covered market.

The first suburban extension flowed along the Exeter Road, along the northern shores of Sutton Pool and as far as the junction with Sutton Road. It has always been called Bretonside, and this is quite certainly the area burnt by the French in 1403. It was a Breton force, which landed at the back of the town, at Cattedown, and fairly certainly never got past Martin's Gate and the town walls. This was commemorated for centuries after by an annual battle between the Breton Boys - the residents of Bretonside - and the Old Town Boys, who had lived inside the walls and not been overrun, though flaming arrows probably burnt down most of their houses. But it is all confused; the street fight was staged on Freedom Day in mid-September when the town boundaries were beaten. When it got too rough for the streets it was moved to Freedom Fields, where the Sabbath Day battle of the Civil War took place. There was, until the late 1970s, a pub on Bretonside called the Burton Boys, a corruption of the name, but it seems odd to call a suburb Bretonside because it had been burnt by the Bretons. Early spellings are Britayne Side, and there are reasons for thinking that the Britons of Bretonside might have been there before the Anglo-Saxons of Sutton.

The original town was on the north side of Notte Street and the Parade inlet. In the fifteenth century houses were being built along Southside Street, but there is evidence so far of only three. The gin distillery is the only surviving building of those days, although its original purpose is still obscure. William Yogge, mayor in 1459, 1461, 1467 and 1470, build a 'great House' on the harbourside not far from the distillery. But it is a hundred years, well into Elizabethan times, before a new street, which is probably Southside Street, was paved in 1582. In 1584 there was trou-

HOUSES, CHURCHES AND PUBS

Left: *a view of Southside Street looking towards the gin distillery. The medieval arch in the foreground and the distillery are evidence of some pre-Elizabethan development on the Southside.*
Above: *A recent photograph of the same stretch of Southside Street.*

ble with surface water coming down from 'Mr Sperkes newe streate.' New Street and Hoegate Street were the limits of these expansions, born of the new Elizabethan wealth, and because in this area the new houses of 1570-1600 have lasted into our own time rather better than the older houses in the medieval town have done, it is often regarded as the oldest corner of the town.

THE TOWN SPREADS

After the seige of Plymouth, which had finally demonstrated that the walls were no longer of use, the town began to flow out over them, though to a very limited extent. There was a slight spread on the Hoe slopes west of Hoegate Street. Another, around what is now the Central Hall, just outside the Old Town Gate, was known as Old Town Without. In the eighteenth century the Bretonside area began to reach up what old Plymothians call Vinegar Hill. As this development was round the new church of Charles (completed in 1658) it was called Charlestown, but it had only climbed to Regent Street by the time of the Prince Regent (1811-20), after whom the street was named.

Plymouth celebrated the jubilee year of George III's reign in 1810 by cutting a new road from the end of Bretonside eastwards to meet the road Lord Boringdon was bringing in from his new Laira embankment and his new Iron Bridge across the Plym. Until then Bretonside halted at the Old Tree, which had stood in the middle of the road since late Elizabethan times, and the way to Exeter was up North Street and Lipson Road. Beyond the Old Tree a maze of houses reached

SUTTON HARBOUR

A 1960 view of Exeter Street, with the Georgian Brunswick Terrace on the right and St John's Church beyond. Brunswick Terrace was demolished soon after the picture was taken and the houses on the left removed to make way for the six-lane highway leading to the Cattedown roundabout.

out to Coxside Corner. The new road, Exeter Street, was cut through this and public houses, the Regent (now the Swallow) and the Jubilee (gone), date from this reconstruction. The severe elegance of Brunswick Terrace, built about 1811, and the softer charm of South Devon Terrace, still visible in spite of the rough treatment it has had, show how the new road was built up as far as Cattedown Corner. The First and Last Inn marks the limit of the built-up area. There was some housing behind Coxside but the name of Alma Street shows that it was mid-century before Cattedown grew, to provide houses for the new industries.

Over the centuries the wealthy, merchants and ship-owners, lived in the houses when they were new, and with nearly every expansion of the town they were the people to move out into the new houses, leaving their old and decaying mansions to go down the social scale. In medieval Plymouth it is clear that the houses which James Barber excavated on the Parade, under the 1970 flats, had quite comfortably-off people living in them. Later excavations before the building in 1992 of Brock House, the sheltered housing at the foot of Batter Street (on the site of the old Mayoralty House), made the pattern clear. The merchants lived on the north side of Vauxhall

HOUSES, CHURCHES AND PUBS

Street with their warehouses stretching out over the harbour on the other side of the street. There were inlets of water between the warehouses which served the merchant ships as little docks from which goods could be unloaded directly into the stores. A similar pattern was found by later excavations before North Quay House was built. Here the houses were on the seaward side of Lower Street with the warehouses built further out over the harbour. Almost all Hawker's Avenue was one of these 'docks', with the tide flowing up what was called the Old Tree Slip almost to Lower Street.

In late Elizabethan times merchants like Page lived in Vauxhall Street, and Southside Street residents provided mayors. A rich merchant like Thomas Yogge had built himself a house by St Andrew's Church before 1500, and by 1550 the Hawkins family had a house in Kinterbury Street, where the bus station is now. Drake had his town house at the bottom of Looe Street and the rich Robert Trelawny of Ham had a house further up Looe Street. All these houses started with gardens which were quickly filled with little cottages for the household servants and workmen; Plymouth's small physical expansion as her population grew in the seventeenth and eighteenth centuries is due to this kind of infilling.

If the very rich moved out to become country gentlemen, the professional and merchant classes still stayed in the main streets round the Barbican. Cookworthy built his house in Notte Street in 1710; it was altered in the last century into a warehouse on the ground floor with a Pentecostal League chapel above (in the 'upper room'). Now it is a restaurant called The Revival. The fine three-storey house whose Georgian redbrick is now masked with yellow paint at No. 12 the Barbican was probably the 'Great House' built by Robert Bayly in the late eighteenth century; when he first came to Plymouth from Poole as a boy of 14 young Bayly, founder of the great Plymouth family, lived with his uncle, Captain Brahaut, at Island House, which is still Bayly property.

Among the Hoe terraces west of Hoegate Street one can still find houses that once stood in their own grounds, built for well-to-do people, and it is the same in Charlestown. Brunswick Terrace had its doctors and professional men in living memory. Isaac Foot lived next to his building business in Notte Street until late in the last century.

UNHEALTHY SLUMS

But behind these main streets the old houses, built with Tudor sanitary arrangements and little improved, went downhill. Some areas were crowded from the start, like the Friary Green area and the lanes behind Exeter Street. When the old castle was destroyed with the building of the

Palace Court, where the merchant Paynter is said to have entertained Katherine of Aragon on her first arrival in England; subsequently her divorce from Henry VIII led to the creation of the Church of England. The building was demolished in 1880 to make way for Palace Court School and the only surviving fragments of the mansion can be seen in a courtyard behind the school.

SUTTON HARBOUR

The slums of the Barbican area; New Street, from a drawing in the City Art Gallery.

Citadel the area was first quarried out, then used as a tip, and then built up with narrow lanes, interlocking courts, and tiny houses.

Between 1801 and 1851 Plymouth's population leapt from 16 000 people to nearly 50 000, mainly through immigration. Part of this was from the distressed agricultural areas of Devon and Cornwall, part from the famine-stricken Ireland, but the Irish who settled moved into the King Street area, living like modern emigrants in a tightly-knit community with little contact with the English. This area produced Plymouth's worst slum, but the lanes off Exeter Street, the Castle Street area, Looe Street and How Street became congested slums. Plymouth had known bad spells of disease before. Apart from the Black Death of 1439 for which no figures survive, the plague had killed 600 in 1579-80 and over 2000 in 1625-6 when the defeated soldiers from Cadiz were left to rot in the town. Cholera struck in 1832, killing 779 people, and again in 1849, killing 819 people. It was a less mortal attack in 1849, when only a quarter of the infected died as against half the infected in 1832. But as the average death rate for the seven years before 1851 was over 23 people in every 1000 the Board of Health ordered an inquiry.

Its report was devastating. Much of it applies to the Sutton Harbour area. 'Plymouth ranks among the most unhealthy towns of Great Britain', it runs. 'The streets inhabited by the poor are narrow, the courts are confined and the houses and room tenements overcrowded... water supply defective and impure (the source was sound but open leats collected every kind of filth), the sewers limited and some faulty, privy accommodation deficient, surface cleaning not properly attended to, the poor overcrowded, ventilation bad.' There were narrow, dirty and overcrowded courts, served by one privy, usually filthy, a cesspit in the middle full and overflowing, one stand pipe with the water turned on for two hours every day.

The Unitarian minister, the Rev. W. J. Odgers, made two detailed surveys of the town. The slum north of the harbour was clearly the worst - 128 people died in Moon Street in one year. In Castle Street, which averaged 12 ft in width and had surface drainage only, 564 people lived at an average of 19 to a house, in 30 houses, 14 of which had no privy or WC. In New Street, which averaged 18 ft in width and had no drainage, 598 people lived at an average of 14 to a house in 43 houses, 26 of which had no privy or WC. Castle Street had only three cholera deaths in 1849 and New Street 17, but these houses and the courts between were rarely free from typhoid. Three rooms in Castle Street each had seven people living in then; in New Street there were five like this but Southside Street had four rooms with eight occupants each. Castle Dyke Lane, linking New Street and Castle Street had six houses 'more like hogsties' and a slaughter house with a large accumulation of dung. It was 6 ft wide, with only surface drainage, and its 146 people lived 24 to a house. Four of the six had no privy or WC. And these were not the worst streets.

THE BEERHOUSES

The Rev. John Hatchard, Vicar of St Andrew's, told the inspector that beer houses (which required no licence and were not controlled at all) swarmed in Plymouth and were the curse of the town, scenes of everything degrading to human nature. Another witness talked of trawler 'apprentices', boys between 10 and 16, who made up to five shillings a week supplying fishermen with bait and spent this 'squid money' in beer houses, each with his prostitute aged between 8 and 12. In many cases boys and girls were not turned out of the beer houses until six or eight in the morning, drunk. From 1846 to 1851 the licensed houses only grew from 137 to 140 but the beershops leapt from 119 to 188. Even worse than the beershops were said to be the 'tiddleywinks', or bunker shop, which did not even have the name of the beer-seller over the door and where people went who were turned out of beershops at 11 p.m.

White's Directory for 1850 details this picture. The licensed houses in Castle Street were the Bunch of Grapes, Fountain, Jolly Young Waterman, Lord Nelson, Rising Sun, Seventeen Stars, and the Welcome Home Sailor. Then there were five beer houses. It was the centre of an area

A courtyard in the warren behind Lambhay Hill; not cleared until the late 1950s.

'noted for debauchery' and although these figures show 12 taverns in the 30 houses, Whitfeld says of Castle Street, or Castle Rag, or Damnation Alley, that 'every house was formerly an inn, and every inn a brothel'. In New Street stood the Anchor and Hope (No. 23), the East and West Country House, the Robin Hood (licensed again but calling itself a cafe-nightclub), the Royal Highlander, and the Welchman's Arms. New Street had no beer houses, at least no listed ones.

The Barbican presented an impressive waterfront in 1850. There was the Admiral McBride (the one folk-hero honoured in the area and dating from about 1800), then across the foot of

SUTTON HARBOUR

The Old Ring of Bells on the corner of Vauxhall Street and Woolster Street, before it was demolished in 1965. Several of the rooms had fine plasterwork ceilings. The office of the Sutton Harbour company is to the left of the pub.

Castle Street the Brunswick, (which changed its name to the Mayflower about 1890-1900 and was a casualty of 1941), the North Country Pink next door, beer houses at Nos. 6 and 10, the Crown and Anchor (which became the Sir Francis Chichester and has changed its name again to the Pilgrims bar-cafe), and the Dolphin, where some of the Tolpuddle Martyrs spent their first night in England on their return from transportation. Southside Street had the Albion, the Clarence, the Maritime and the Navy.

RESPECTABLE TAVERNS

Not all these places must be damned as sinks of iniquity. The Navy, for instance, appears to have been built by Ralph Ord in 1786 on land leased from the Duchy, and was not only a property of the Sutton Harbour company until they sold it in 1901, but in 1822 housed the offices of the company. The Mitre went in 1811 to make way for the Exchange (which in turn went in the Blitz) and the Old Ring of Bells with its plaster ceilings from Tudor times was long derelict before it was removed after the war to widen the Vauxhall Street-Woolster Street corner. The King's Arms at Old Tree was the principal coaching house and the scene of mayoral dinners before the building of the Royal Hotel in 1812, and Lucien, Napoleon Bonaparte's brother, stayed there in 1810 when he fell out with his brother (five years later the Emperor himself was in Plymouth Sound, a prisoner, but he never came ashore). The King's Arms shrank away to be replaced by the Bretonside council flats in 1935, and the same fate met the Prince George in Vauxhall Street, where a young naval officer, Prince William Henry, was initiated as a freemason into Lodge No. 86 in 1786. The Prince spent much of his naval service in the Three Towns and was very popular; his later title of Duke of Clarence constantly crops up and as King William IV he probably knew Plymouth better than any English monarch before or since. Early Masonic history also tells us about the inns of the eighteenth century. Lodge of Sincerity (No. 189) was formed at the Three Crowns on the Parade in 1796. This inn still has an eighteenth-century facade of some elegance but its back dates from about 1600. It is usually accepted that the Minerva in Looe Street is the oldest building in Plymouth to house a pub. The Ship Inn, opposite the Three Crowns, dates from the later half of the eighteenth century.

But if pubs with splendid names like the Sign of the Topsail Mast Block, which was on the Parade in 1746, and the Sawyers Arms in the former Salt House on Old Tree Slip in 1817 have gone, many survive. An 1822 list of the principal inns of Plymouth includes the Maritime Inn, the Navy Inn, and the Three Crowns. Pubs which survive from the 1850 directory include the Fisherman's Arms in Lambhay Street, the King's Head on Bretonside, and the Potters and Shipwrights Arms beside Marrowbone Slip. In 1823 this pub was just the Potters; then it added shipwrights to its title by 1850, showing the

HOUSES, CHURCHES AND PUBS

industrial changes, and now it is simply the Shipwrights. It is the only pub still owned by the Sutton Harbour Company. The fine building of the Marine Hotel in Queen Anne's Place was there in 1850 and survives, but is no longer licensed. The vanished Jersey and Guernsey Packet which was on Sutton Wharf is another reminder of an old trading link.

NEW PARISHES

The Church of England was early in the fight against the slums. Both St Andrew's and Charles first moved to help the children and, as Charles was closest to the waterfront and probably had the poorest houses in its area, it was first off the mark. The Rev. Robert Hawker, grandfather of the eccentric poet-priest Hawker of Morwenstow, was a curate there for a long time before he became vicar in 1784. Within three years he had started a Sunday School, the first in Plymouth, meeting in Friary Court and then the Mitre in Woolster Street before the Household of Faith was built in Vennel Street. The first purpose-built Sunday School in England, it disappeared to make way for the Charles roundabout. Hawker's successor as vicar, the Rev. James Carne, died with his wife in tending the sick in the cholera outbreak of 1832.

The Vicar of St Andrew's from 1824 to 1870, the Rev. John Hatchard built Holy Trinity Church in Southside Street as a chapel-at-ease in 1840-2. Actually the Sunday School faced Southside Street next to the Queen's Arms pub. The site is now occupied by the new block in front of the Blackfriars photocopiers and printers. The church, which seated 1200 people, was behind and at right angles, with its entrance in Friar's Lane facing the fine Georgian house, No. 3, which became the vicarage. It is described as 'a neat

Looking down Looe Street before 1895; the right-hand building is now an arts centre.

High Street in the 1880s, with the Naval Reserve Inn on the right, and the Napoleon Inn looking down the street. All this has made way for the wide road called Buckwell Street climbing from Notte Street to the Guild of Community Service office.

73

SUTTON HARBOUR

Holy Trinity, the Barbican's parish church was destroyed in the bombing of 1941. Through the windows of the ruins, since demolished, can be seen the Queen Anne house, which became a solicitor's office, on the opposite side of Friar's Lane. The north wall of the ruins still stands in Blackfriar Print's car park.

Doric building'. Behind that again, reaching to Citadel Road on the site of the present Masonic Hall, were Holy Trinity Schools. All this big complex survived and was at work until destroyed by bombs in 1941. Now just one wall remains of the church, at the end of the Blackfriars printing firm's car park. In 1851 the old parishes were carved up to create five new ones. Holy Trinity became literally the parish church of the Barbican area in 1851 and its first vicar, the Rev. Francis Barnes, became a terror of the wrongdoers. He would roam Damnation Alley of a night, breaking in on men and women dancing naked in the brothel-inns and shame them with his denunciations; he attacked the worst of the tiddleywinks and the beer houses until some of their operators fled from his wrath leaving even their furniture behind them.

But as fast as Parson Barnes closed down the beer houses so they filled up with people. The population of Plymouth rose from 53 000 in 1851 to 68 000 in 1871. Holy Trinity parish alone had 4886 people, in an area that must have been bounded roughly by the harbour, the Parade, Notte Street and Windsor Lane (the present Armada Way). So Holy Trinity itself built a chapel-of-ease, St Saviour's, at the top of Lambhay Hill. Its site was described as the glacis of the Citadel and the Queen gave the land. Private subscriptions paid for the building but they did not run to an architect. So Parson Barnes (who was also chaplain to the Emigration Depot) turned his hand to that as well, and his tower still dominates Lambhay Hill though the church was removed for new housing after the war. St Saviour's with its 380 seats was opened in 1870, became a parish in its own right and only reunited with Holy Trinity just before the war. Now both parishes are back in St Andrew's.

The eastern part of Charles parish became the parish of St John Sutton-on-Plym, built in 1854. In spite of the strong evangelical outlook of both St Andrew's and Charles, St John's (like St Peter's at the western end of the town) came under the Puseyite influence and still has a strong High Church flavour. But if the Anglicans could split fiercely on dogma and ceremony, they put equal and fervent zeal into their work for the poor. Charles was not content with the Household of Faith or its day schools, it took a Sunday School right into Moon Street, the worse area between Ebrington Street and Exeter Street, and held Sunday evening mission services there too.

FREE CHURCH MISSIONS

Nor were the free churches behind. The Bethel Union, largely supported in its early days by Methodist and Independent churches, launched a mission to seamen and opened a chapel right in Castle Street itself, in 1833. Again a large day school and Sunday School were an integral part of the work. But its primary target was the sol-

HOUSES, CHURCHES AND PUBS

diers, sailors and fishermen who used the area. A library, canteen and cheap meals, a recreation room and a famous penny saving-scheme were all part of its enterprises, and at one time the Bethel had such influence that it stopped Sunday fishing out of the harbour. In 1883 a new building was erected at the bottom of Castle Street. The Bethel Mission went in the 1970s. At the top of the steps from the Barbican one used to enter a very Victorian mission chapel; now it is a restaurant and the Barbican Theatre has taken over the Sunday School hall from the amateur theatre group, the Tamaritans. The Cattewater Commissioners and the pilots occupy the building on the Barbican.

On the other side of the harbour is a formal limestone building with its entrance in Harbour Avenue but its gable end right on Exeter Street, which at that point carries six lanes of traffic in and out of the city. It was originally built in 1779 by the Wesleyans, as the Lower Street Chapel, and John Wesley himself preached there a few years after its opening. In 1845, when the Baptists were moving their main church into George Street, they bought the Lower Street premises and maintained it as a mission church in what was rapidly becoming a slum area. The facade was rebuilt in 1882 and the mission flourished, at one time having 400 pupils and 35 teachers in its Sunday School. Slum clearance in the 1930s

The Household of Faith, the eighteenth-century Sunday School built by Charles Church. It was demolished to make way for the south side of the roundabout encircling the church.

Lower Street Mission Hall (left) in its last days as a place of worship. Mariner's Court now replaces the storehouses roofed with corrugated iron, and Exeter Street in the foreground has been widened yet again.

reduced the population, but it continued after the war as an evangelical centre. When this ceased in 1958 attempts were made to run the mission as a centre for the unemployed. These efforts collapsed and in 1986 the building was sold and converted into offices.

Until 1941 an iron sign arched over the entrance to a narrow alleyway in Bretonside, opposite the Salvation Army Hall and the pedestrian crossing. It bore the letters 'Tabernacle'. At the end of the alleyway stood the Old Tabernacle, built in 1745 by Andrew Kinsman in the garden of his Bretonside shop and used for nonconformist worship. When Kinsman died his son fell out with the congregation who built themselves the New Tabernacle in Norley Street, from which eventually sprang Sherwell Church. After various uses the Old Tabernacle was taken over in 1884 by the North Quay Working Men's Mission Band. It was finally destroyed in the bombing of 1941.

In Sutton Road, leading out to Coxside, a building with a gable prominently dated 1905 on the corner of Clare Place was the Clare Mission. Members of Sherwell Congregational Church had first rented and then bought cottages there which were eventually replaced with the hall, built on the site in 1905. It was damaged in the blitz but restored, and went on until dwindling attendances brought its closure in 1960.

Other churches maintained missions in the poor areas around Sutton Harbour. For the Anglicans, St Andrew's started in Kinterbury Street in 1879, and three years later opened the Lower Lane Mission. The first Sunday School opened in 1883, by 1885 the Mission opened a purpose-built mission hall in Palace Street which was called St Thomas's, and this flourished until after the Second World War. Later a store for Michael Newman, the antique dealer, the hall is still there, its entrance facing the new Sir John Hawkins Square. St Simon's had its mission hall in Notte Street. The Roman Catholics were on the edge of the harbour area in Holy Cross, opened in 1882 and just a few minutes from North Quay. The Methodist churches in Ebrington Street (one a wartime casualty and the other, Wesley, built in 1877, was destroyed by fire in 1936) were close to poor areas. Wesley's large Sunday School in North Street was surrounded by slums.

General Booth brought the Salvation Army banner to Plymouth early in his campaign but its first corps in Plymouth was founded in 1878 off Union Street. The second corps in 1882 was located in How Street until old Isaac Foot built the hall in Exeter Street for them, his only contract with the Army being a shake of the hand. They took colour and life to the poor and, like the other denominations, gave them courage and help when they could. The Exeter Street corps opened this hall in 1920, had it destroyed in the Blitz, rebuilt in 1952, and finally sold when the corps took over the former Methodist church at Whitleigh in 1996.

Not all the wretched people in the quarter were vicious. Most were unfortunate victims of the poverty of the times, driven from the rural districts by the farming depression into a town that could not grow fast enough to house them. The churches could offer spiritual help and try to redeem those depraved by poverty. But physical help was needed, in housing and sanitation, and here the great work of the churches was in stirring the conscience of the town.

CONCERN FOR HEALTH

The Corporation had, for instance, bought buildings in Hoegate Street in 1848 for washhouses but left them idle. Mr Odgers, the Unitarian minister, raised voluntary subscriptions to convert the buildings and they opened as washhouses in 1850. In the first three years they catered for an average of 8500 bathers a year but not until 1855, when Mr Odgers had left Plymouth, did the Corporation take them over. The premises were rebuilt in the 1930s and finally closed in 1974 because of dwindling use.

The Plymouth Public Dispensary was started in 1789 at the old Mayoralty House in Woolster Street. (Brock House, flats for old people, was built on the site, the corner of Batter Street, in 1993). The only remnant of the Mayoralty House, the old granite doorway, has been rebuilt by the Barbican Association in their Elizabethan Garden in New Street. The Dispensary built its own premises in Catherine Street in 1809, which still survives. In 1831 moves were made to build a hospital and in 1840 the South Devon and East Cornwall Hospital was opened on the south side of Notte Street, in what had formerly been cherry gardens. Not until 1884 was it replaced by Greenbank Hospital and the Notte Street building was sold.

It was rebuilt as a repository for Spooners, about which one story should be told: after some bomb damage during the war the managing director of Spooners, John Bedford, had a strongroom inspected and in it found Drake's Drum, sent for safe keeping after a fire at Buckland Abbey a few years before. He insisted that it be sent back at once to the Abbey. That very night the repository was bombed and burnt out.

In its hospital days the building at best had only 105 beds, and Plymouth was then approaching 100 000 population.

One result of the 1852 Health Inquiry was that in 1855 Plymouth Corporation adopted the Public Health Act, becoming a Local Board of Health and taking over the work of the old Board of Improvement Commissioners. Notte Street, Woolster Street and Hoegate Street were widened and some of the worst houses were pulled down. But no new ones were built and people were still pouring into the town; the increase by migration in the years 1851-71 alone was 10 000 and the total population had risen by 18 000. In 1872 a smallpox epidemic hit the town, so badly that the remedy of Elizabethan times had to be applied, a temporary wooden hospital built in the fields at Greenbank. Smallpox had ravaged Plymouth many times in the century but this was the worst attack; hundreds died and the newspapers were persuaded not to publish the daily death roll, to prevent panic.

Old cottages in Pin Lane, long demolished.

Clare Buildings in Coxside; still occupied in 1965. These 1890s 'artisan dwellings' were private enterprise slum clearance known as 'five per cent philanthropy' after the profit the developers took from their investment.

In 1880 Henry Whitfeld wrote a series of articles in the *Western Daily Mercury* pointing out that Plymouth, the seventh most unhealthy town in England in 1852, was now the third worst in the country for overcrowding. He toured the town and found in the poor quarters that the general rule was one room, one family, sometimes three generations. The house at the entrance to Cooksley's Court, off Castle Street, had 60 people in it, and it was not unique. All the women in the courts took in washing, much from the ships in harbour, importing all kinds of disease. The tumble-down houses and appalling sanitary conditions were no better than those in the 1853 report. It was no good tearing down these houses, he argued, unless new ones were built. A start had been made by private individuals and though they offered no more than one room, one family, for the people could afford no more, the barrack-like buildings of the Artisans Dwellings Company, or Sir Edward Bates and John Pethick's 'Artisans Dwellings', in Notte Street and Coxside and off St Andrew's Street with their iron staircases and balconies did give them light and air, a sound roof and sanitation. The businessmen who invested their money in these buildings were sneered at as '5 per cent philanthropists', but their intervention did help the poor.

THE TOWN ACTS

The Corporation brought the drainage to better standards, began its housing for working classes with Shaftesbury Cottages, and an estate at Prince Rock. In 1890 the Mayor, Mr J. T. Bond, led a slumming tour which resulted in the north side of Looe Street being condemned and the present Corporation houses there were opened in 1898. A choice story is told that Queen Victoria's Diamond Jubilee was celebrated with a great bonfire on the Hoe, built of timber from the condemned Looe Street and How Street houses. The Mayor and aldermen and councillors with their families all had the front seats; when the flames bit into the ancient timbers all their insect population flew for shelter, to the complete discomfort of the civic dignitaries.

But replacing the slums was a slow process. By 1919 only 420 new dwellings had been built by the town. There was another push between the wars and by 1937 another 3133 new Council dwellings had been added. The main development was at Swilly but the older blocks of flats in Lambhay Street, Castle Dyke Lane, New Street, Stokes Lane, Buckwell Street, Moon Street, Hill Street, and Teat's Hill date from this time.

In this attack on the slums Mr Southcombe

Parker, an architect who had made a most valuable survey of the old houses round the harbour, successfully fought to preserve 32 New Street. Now known as the Elizabethan House, it receives thousands of visitors each year. The people who rescued it formed themselves into the Old Plymouth Society.

The last drive against the slums, which started in 1957 and finally eradicated sub-standard housing from all the area round Sutton Harbour, also threatened to destroy houses which had been reprieved and repaired thirty years before. Eventually the Plymouth Barbican Association took over and restored the best of the old houses. The Corporation cleared the unlamented Castle Street area and rebuilt with a most attractive mixture of houses in traditional style, keeping the feel of cobbled lanes and old courts running up the hill, still watched over by Parson Barnes's tower at the top.

In between was Castle Street School, a towered and attractive product of the Education Act of 1870. The Anglicans already had their day schools in the area; Charles (1838), St Andrew's (1842), Holy Trinity (1844). Now the School Board could move and one can see where the need was; King Street and Treville Street Schools were built in 1872, Castle Street and Sutton Road in 1873, Palace Court in 1880. Though over a century old, most of the buildings still survive, although the dwindling number of young families from the area meant they stopped being primary schools. Treville Street became the thriving Martin's Gate Secondary Modern School; others like Palace Court and Sutton Road became departments of the College of Art.

This is fitting enough, for by the 1970s the harbour area was becoming fashionable to live in and the artist were the first to arrive. They took rooms in houses where habitation was not permitted and, with mattresses in corners, played cat and mouse games with sanitary and housing inspectors. Now this phase has passed; there is considerable range of studios and craft workshops; many of the artists have found accepted living quarters in the area and, after the early suspicions of the indigenous population, are now accepted and welcomed. When the painter, Robert Lenkiewicz, decorated the blank back of a store overlooking the Parade with a huge mural of Elizabethan times (now covered) he used Barbican people as models and enlisted boys of the neighbourhood as watchdogs against vandals. Behind the artists have come professional people of all kinds, and there is a great demand for living accommodation by people willing to pay good rents.

One cannot replace slop shops and instrument shops with antique dealers and restaurants, or sawdust bars for fishermen with tarted-up brewer's suburban, without some loss of character. But by and large the improvers have been careful; the area still has a healthy vitality. No one who can remember the squalid hovels, the drunkenness, the women fighting with hatpins outside the pubs of a Saturday night, would wish for it back. We may regret some of the historic houses that have gone, but reading Odgers and Whitfeld is to be persuaded that there was little real choice.

FAMOUS MEN

Yet rough and tough as the area was, it has produced many fine people in all walks of life, and some remarkable characters.

There was John Kitto, the deaf son of a mason born in Stillman Street in 1804, who became a missionary and a great bible scholar. The boys' club which the YMCA ran in the street from 1892 until 1972 (when the building was demolished for

The Merchant's House in St Andrew's Street as it was: on the left is the Swan Hotel.

SUTTON HARBOUR

Local spirit is still strong; children's sports on West Pier during a 1970s Sutton Harbour regatta week.

road widening) was named after him, and the name was kept by the YMCA for their new centre at Honicknowle, serving new housing estates. In turn the school across the road took the name of John Kitto Community College.

Two years younger than Kitto was Robert White Stevens; born in Southside Street in 1806, a son of John Stevens who was a ship-owner running schooners in the fruit trade. Robert Stevens founded the Parade Printing Works and was the Plymouth correspondent of *The Times*; as such he got news from ships making their first English calls at Plymouth (it was before radio) and for the important stories he would hire a special train to rush the information to London. But he is chiefly remembered as the author of *Stevens on Stowage*, a book on ship-loading that was a seaman's bible for many years and is still regarded as a classic. His brother, Thomas, who took over the family shipping business, was Mayor in 1854 and Thomas's grandson, Marshall Stevens, was the moving spirit behind the building of the Manchester Ship Canal, its first general manager, and then the creator and managing director of the Trafford Park Industrial Estate at Manchester. The name of Marshall Stevens's father, Sanders Stevens, is preserved in the name of the shipping agents.

Sir Joseph Bellamy was a Barbican boy whom Luscombe, the great shipping agent, took on as a clerk and who rose to inherit the firm (which still bears his name), became chairman of the Sutton Harbour Improvement Company, Mayor of Plymouth, and a knight. Isaac Foot was a Horrabridge carpenter who set up as a builder in Notte Street. His fourth son, another Isaac, became a solicitor, Member of Parliament, Minister of the Crown, and Lord Mayor of Plymouth; three of the second Isaac's sons, Lord Caradon, Sir Dingle and Michael have been Cabinet Ministers and Michael also had a spell as Leader of the Labour Party in Opposition. The only one who remained faithful to the Liberal Party, John, became a life peer as Lord Foot of Buckland Monachorum. Stanley Gibbons started his stamp-dealing business in Treville Street; Farley's Rusks were invented in a shop in Exeter Street in 1878.

The list is long. And for every single estimable character who emerged to make his mark on Plymouth life, there are hundreds of decent, honest, anonymous citizens of Plymouth still who are proud of their Barbican background. Southside Street and Exeter Street were to some extent two village streets, and those old community loyalties are neither dead nor forgotten.

CHAPTER 8
WORK ASHORE

For both the merchants and the working men round Sutton Harbour the basic way of earning a living was fishing or seafaring, and those who chose not to go to sea worked on the quaysides, and in the warehouses. Then there are the traditional trades. Refining salt is one of the oldest. The Salt House beside Old Tree Slip, now called Hawkers Avenue, named after the wine merchant, had become the Sawyer's Arms by 1817 but a salt house on Bretonside, its back premises reaching back to the tidemark before North Quay was built, survived until 1867. Snow and Ogg can be traced as owners, and at the end it was known as Skardon's Salt House.

Like every town in the days before easy transport, Plymouth made most of the goods that it required, and these little manufactories were boosted in the seventeenth and eighteenth centuries by an extra market in the raw and developing settlements of America and the West Indies. In turn the imports from these places led to new industries in the town. Tobacco was made up, one establishment being an old house in Notte Street called the Stone-in-Darns. Clay pipes were also made in a couple of places near the harbour, one on Bretonside. An archaeological party searching for signs of the old castle when Castle Street was pulled down to make way for the modern flats found instead the seventeenth-century town tip. It was littered with broken clay pipes, and yielded so many fragments of pottery from half the countries of Europe, brought in by sea and sold to the Plymouth households, that it is the richest collection of its kind in the country.

The fish market produced work for many hundreds of people. This picture, taken at the turn of the century, shows men and women cleaning fish.

PLYMOUTH GIN

Coates have been making Plymouth Gin in the Black Friars distillery in Southside Street since 1793. Gin-making in the town is older than that; there is a reference to 'the strength of Plymouth water' served at a dinner party earlier in the eighteenth century. Plymouth had welcomed Dutch

SUTTON HARBOUR

Above: *The great copper stills dating from 1855-6 in which Plymouth Gin is distilled; a photograph taken in the days when the Coates family owned the distillery in Southside Street.*

Above right: *The offices of Colliers, the wine merchants in Southside Street, now Wm E. Fox-Smith's antique print and engravings shop.*

settlers since the fifteenth century, with their gin tradition, and one would hesitate to put a foundation date on the trade. Nor were Coates the only distillers; in the last century there were at least two others in Plymouth. But Coates have preserved their special mixture of juniper and other berries, and in the days when it was a family concern and the principal lived just across Blackfriars Lane, in the fine house destroyed in the Blitz, he would cross to inspect the great copper vats (which still operate) at any crucial hour of the night. Since 1945 the firm has been owned by various international companies, but in 1996 it was bought by Plymouth men who restored the ordinary bottles of gin to 40% strength, and changed the name of the firm back to Coates.

Of the harbourside wine merchants who survived the Second World War, Colliers were established in Southside Street in 1676 and their port was already renowned when Captain Marryat was at sea as midshipman with Lord Cochrane. When Marryat turned author he made Peter Simple cry for a bottle of Collier's port for a toast. The company was eventually bought by Dingles and has now vanished; its splendid old offices with their sand-blasted glass panels in the office doors have been occupied since 1981 by William Fox-Smith who sells antiquarian prints and engravings.

Across the harbour on Bretonside were the wine cellars of Hawkers, founded in 1808 although the family was dealing in wine and timber long before that time.

Colonel John Hawker was the first American consul in Plymouth, appointed in 1790. Like Colliers, they preserved the old wine links with Portugal and they were shippers of some wines which first became popular when the Duke of Wellington's army wintered behind the lines of Torres Vedras.

Now Hawkers too have vanished, their old offices in Bretonside are given over to civil engineers, architects and solicitors and their cellars in Hawkers Avenue replaced in 1987 by a block of flats, Harbourside Court.

The last brewery near the harbour was Scott's (Robert Falcon Scott of the Antarctic was a son of the last brewer). Over its yard entrance in Hoegate Street was ironwork depicting a sunrise (it was the Sun Brewery). When the premises were taken over by old Isaac Foot (strong Methodist and teetotaller) he brought up his family in the house in front, in Notte Street, and the way into his builder's yard was under the sunrise sign of the brewery. Now house, yard and sign, on the corner, opposite Age Concern, have all disappeared.

A number of inns brewed their own beer. The Pope's Head, a famous meeting place at the top of Looe Street, was one and the distinctive ventilator roof of a malt-house can still be seen behind the Arts Centre, whose house was next door to the Pope's Head. Pitt's malt-house, at the foot of Looe Street, was in business until the 1960s.

COOKWORTHY

When Cookworthy launched his famous Plymouth porcelain in 1768 he found a ready market in America; indeed his first clue to china clay came from a Quaker who had been prospecting for mines in the back of Virginia and found 'china earth'. Cookworthy too was a Quaker and entertained this man in his Notte Street house, where he was shown some of the American china made from this clay. Cookworthy eventually found some china clay in west Cornwall and, by trial and error, succeeded in making the first true hard-paste porcelain ever made in England. He set up a factory at Coxside in 1768, taking over for this purpose the old victualling storehouses whose last government use, as a hospital, had ended with the building of the Royal Naval Hospital at Stonehouse seven years earlier.

Cookworthy built up a business employing fifty or sixty people but he was a man of 63 when he started it, the products tended to be uneven in their firing, and the wood for fuel was expensive. In 1774, nearly seventy, he sold his patents to an old friend, Richard Champion, who moved the factory to Bristol. Three years later the patent was sold to a Staffordshire group, and in 1780 the old man died. Apart from the China House, he had a shop in Notte Street which sold his products and probably another in the High Street, but he is remembered by inscription below the windows of The Revival, a restaurant in Notte Street which, (though rebuilt as a mission hall in 1883 and again after bomb damage in 1941) is substantially his house. Though he was born in Kingsbridge, Cookworthy spent all his working life in Plymouth and numbered the great among his friends. Captain Cook was often a guest at Notte Street, and Josiah Banks, the most eminent scientist of his day, was a visitor before the first great voyage with Cook. Admiral Sir John Jervis, Earl

William Cookworthy's house in Notte Street, converted in the nineteenth century to two dwellings. Later Issac Foot the builder converted it, carving a grocery store from the ground floor with the evangelical Pentecostal League meeting in 'an upper chamber'. In the 1990s it was converted again, into a restaurant, The Revival.

St Vincent, was a close friend who declared that 'whoever was in Mr Cookworthy's company was always wiser and better for having been in it'.

WOOLLEN FIRM

Coxside at the time that the China House was in use was almost rustic. William Shepherd, whose grandfather greatly extended the woollen industry in Plymouth about the beginning of the eighteenth century, build himself a house at the junction of Sutton Road and St John's Bridge Road. When Mr Shepherd lived there he could look across the virtually untouched Coxside Creek and the green slopes of Teat's Hill with just a couple old houses on it (one is still there) to the open waters of the Sound. His woollen business employed 4000 in a radius of 25 miles and he had half a dozen small ships to run his goods up to the Thames and tranship direct to the East Indiamen off Gravesend. He built a quay on the north bank of Coxside Creek, still called Shepherd's Wharf, and it cannot have damaged his view to look through the rigging of his own little craft moored there.

Most of the woollen mills were on the line of the waste leat, roughly from the University buildings at Drake Circus to Woolworths in New George Street, but one was established at Coxside where another seventy men were employed making the sheepskins into glove leather, with another dozen making glue from the offal. Glue was also made from the bones discarded by the Victually Yard, after the gulls had picked them clean on Marrowbone Slip. There was also a 'foot-oil' manufactory nearby, and the bones on the beach are also explained as a waste product from the factory.

Apart from the East India trade, much of the Plymouth baize and serge went to North America, the ships bringing back tar and turpentine which were processed for use in the shipyards. The American War of Independence brought a big decline to all this business, and the move north of industry in the mechanical revolution which followed finished it off. Shepherd's house became a nunnery, housing Poor Clares who had fled from France, from 1813 to 1834. They called it Clare House, a name remembered still in Clare Street which faced the site of Shepherd's house.

Glue-making survived into the nineteenth century, moving out to Cattedown where its smell is still remembered by older Plymothians. The imports of masts and timber from North America was revived after the War of Independence and even accelerated in the Napoleonic War. The Plymouth & Oreston Timber Company, founded by the Baylys of Island House and whose name was preserved when it merged into the Bayly-Bartlett Group, was established before 1770 in Coxside Creek where the name of Bayly's Wharf still survives.

Seasoning spars at Marrowbone Slip: a raft of timber of the Plymouth & Oreston Timber Company.

WORK ASHORE

The timber company ended up on the China House Wharf until it was finally closed in 1992. Its timber was used in house-building rather than ships, but this trade is as old as the ship-building it replaced at the China House.

Sand for building was landed at the Sand Hard, close to China House, by barges which used to sail up to Laira at high tide and dry out on the mud. Then at low water the crew would climb over the side, shovel aside the mud and fill the hold with 25 to 30 tons of sand. They would sail back to the Sand Hard where horses and carts would be driven to the side of the beached barges at low tide, and the sand shovelled into the carts.

SHIPBUILDING

The earliest reference to ship building in Sutton Pool is in the days of the Black Prince, when the shipwrights building a warship for him went on strike. Ships were built down through the centuries but not until after the Napoleonic Wars is there much knowledge of the yards. During the long war the principal work had been repairing ships and 300 men were at work in the yards in 1814. After the war came nearly a century of building new tonnage. For most of that time there were three yards in the harbour, Moore's where the North East Quay now is, Shilston's at China House and Gent's at Teat's Hill. Just outside the harbour Joseph Banks had a big yard at Queen Anne's Battery, and his docks and slips are still used by the University. Shilston was in business by 1823. Gent and Kerswill (also at Coxside) by 1830, but at that time Banks's yard was at Mutton Cove, Devonport.

Four generations of Moores built ships in Sutton Harbour and the family tree describes the founder (1682-1742) as a shipwright. The family took over the two shipyards on either side of Meeting House Slip, in the north-eastern corner of the harbour, which the 1786 plan (see Page 48) describes as having been built and leased respectively by Mr Barnacott and Messrs Kerswell & Brinel. Joseph Moore was there by 1812. He was followed before 1847 by his nephew William Foster Moore, who was Mayor for the three years 1874-7 and was married in 1876. The family house was right out on the quay at the end of Friary Street and, soon after marrying, Moore moved to North Friary House, in Greenbank Terrace, because the area round his old home was fast becoming a slum. It is a family tradition that he also gave up shipbuilding about this time because he would have nothing to do with iron ships. But the building of North East Quay (opened in 1879) covered his slipway and building dock. Kerswell, who seems to have been displaced at Friary by the Moores, was still in business at Coxside in 1830 and 1850.

The biggest ship ever built in Sutton Harbour, the Earl of Devon; launched by Shilston in 1869 from the China House slips. From a portrait by Percy Dalton.

85

Shilston, at China House Yard had another large yard. In August 1858 he launched a floating dry dock, the first in the west of England. It was 150 ft long and 40 ft wide, capable of taking ships up to 800 tons. Normally moored in Marrowbone Slip, the floating dock was taken to the deepest parts of the harbour, flooded to take the ship for repair, then pumped out and towed back into the slip. Eleven years later Shilston built the biggest craft ever launched in the harbour, the *Earl of Devon*, 146 ft long, 28 ft beam and 16 ft 6 in draught.

The yard was famous for turning out fast fishing trawlers of which the best remembered was the *Erycina*, PH 63, a 46 tonner built in 1882 and cutter-rigged; converted to a ketch in about 1894 and burnt on the beach in 1946. In 22 trawler races in Plymouth *Erycina* took 15 first prizes, 4 second and 2 third prizes. She was frequently matched against the *Ibex* of Brixham, built by Uphams, but *Ibex's* extra 3 ft on the waterline gave her the title of 'the fastest trawler in the Westcountry'. *Erycina* had a fishing life over fifty years, and when she was laid up her lines were taken off and are now in the National Maritime Museum, with both sail plans.

Sutton Harbour ships were normally less than 100 tons up to the Crimean War, but the impetus given to shipbuilding then increased the size up to 1000 tons. Moore for instance in the 1860s launched the *Falcon* and the *Lily of Devon* which made good times home from Canton with tea, and Shilston's 1863 *Island Maid* of 210 tons went into the Mediterranean fruit trade. Sutton Harbour ships were long-lived; Shilston's 233 ton *Countess of Devon* for instance, built in 1873, was lost going into Liverpool in a storm on the night of 13 November 1907. A full study of Plymouth shipbuilding has yet to be made but Grahame Farr's tables, extracted from Custom House ship registers for the ports from Milford round the coast to Bridport, show that Plymouth had the third largest number of registrations between 1824 and 1835, only beaten by Brixham and Bristol, and easily led the field from 1836 to 1899. All told 2,926 ships were registered in Plymouth in that period, and while that does not necessarily reflect the number of ships built in the port it may well be a guide. Some ships built in Plymouth were for owners in other ports; Plymouth owners were also registering in their home port ships build for them in Prince Edward Island. There were 14 of these vessels registered in 1831, 19 in 1841, and 15 in 1846, sample figures extracted by Basil Greenhill.

The shipbuilders were also owners, Shilstons usually put 'Devon' into the name of their craft, such as *Rose of Devon* and *Girl of Devon*. Their fleet began in the Newfoundland trade and later ranged the world for general cargo. Shilston's last schooner, the *Western Lass*, was carrying china clay as late as 1927 when she was wrecked off Sennen Cove. The South Devon Shipping Company, which had its offices and cellars on Custom House Quay, ran a little fleet of schooners from London round to Bristol until late in the century. John Westcott & Co., still in the coal business in the port, built up another fleet of small craft, of which several were built at Salcombe, and the last, *My Lady* (the 'My' prefix was a Westcott mark), was laid up in Plymouth in 1930, became a houseboat at Salcombe and was only broken up in Plymouth just before the Second World War.

Shipbreaking by Demellweek & Redding replaced shipbuilding at Marrowbone Slip. One of the Great Western tenders, the *Sir Francis Drake*, was broken up there in 1954 but the most famous craft to come to an end on this beach was H.M.S. *Amethyst*, of Yangtse River fame, in 1957.

WORK ASHORE

HMS Amethyst *of Yangtze River fame, being broken up on Marrowbone Slip in 1957. Behind the lamp-post is the China House, in its pre-pub days.*

The last repair firm in the harbour, Fox & Haggart on Sutton Wharf, was founded in 1930. In 1968 the firm employed forty men and dealt with 250 vessels totalling 175 000 tons. Since 1969, when Willoughbys in Millbay Dock closed, they are the last boiler makers & marine engineers in the port.

SUPPORT TRADE

Not only did this extensive ship-building lead to a number of ancillary industries, but the products of these industries also nurtured the young ship-building yards across the Atlantic. Varnish, pitch, and linseed oil were all made at various times, and much was exported to Newfoundland. Like most manufactures this was done at Coxside, for at the beginning of the nineteenth century this was the only undeveloped land left close to the harbour. Making barrels in which ships could carry their provisions required a cooperage, and Lethbridges went into business in 1800. When barrels were no longer needed they acquired a large supply of timber from an old wooden wall being broken up, and began making garden furniture and souvenirs. On the writer's desk at the moment are Lethbridge book-ends in teak from the *Queen Elizabeth*, Beatty's flagship in 1917. In the late 1960s they sold their cooperage on Sutton Wharf to the Improvement Company and moved to Yealmpton.

In 1814 fourteen ropewalks employed 170 people. A man literally walked backwards ravelling the ropes, and long narrow places were needed. One stretched almost the whole length of Teat's Hill Road for most of last century and for at least fifty years a covered ropewalk stretched alongside Embankment Road, only removed when Embankment Road Methodist Church was built. Henry Pope & Co., who took over the Teat's Hill ropewalk from Rodds early in the century, owned much of the land from there out to Queen Anne's Battery. They had close family links with the Pope shipbuilders at Turnchapel and in Prince Edward Island, and a finger in every kind of shipping pie: owners, builders, agents, and sail makers.

Most canvas and sail-cloth making had been done in Mill Lane, beside the woollen mills, but the last firm in this line of business, that of R. B. Tope & Co. on Southside Street, had a different origin. The first Mr Tope, a baker in the Union and Castle ships (both lines called at Plymouth regularly) came ashore and founded a bakery in a corner of the Parade. He lent tents to Holy Trinity for Sunday School outings, and in time had to find sailmakers to mend the tents. From this the tent business so grew that in 1880 he turned from baker to tent-maker. The Nash brothers ran their fruit wholesalers business next to the original Tope bakery; their great-grandfather was a mate in a topsail schooner in the Mediterranean fruit trade who married a Plymouth girl, came ashore and started the fruit business. His son, James L. Nash also built up the Channel Islands potato trade and with his wife (a daughter of the first Isaac Foot) founded the Pentecostal League, an evangelical movement, in Cookworthy's house in Notte Street. A gantry (now removed) was specially built on Sutton Wharf to transport potatoes across the road into the warehouse (which is now Dolphin Court, a block of flats).

POTTERY

But the nineteenth century saw most development on the Coxside shore. The making of coarse pottery, rather like the better-known brown Barnstaple earthenware, went on in three potteries run respectively by Fills, Alger, and Hellyer, the latter's works continuing until the 1870s. From 1810 to 1863 a better kind of china, 'Queen's Ware', in white with blue decoration was made off and on at Coxside. The founder, William Alsop, went to Swansea for a time but later returned and a Staffordshire potter took over on his death. The Queen's Ware seems to have come from the large pottery marked on Brunel's 1845 map, which has been replaced by the Thistle Park Tavern and the long building now occupied by a tyre company, running back to the former gas works gate. Cookworthy's Plymouth porcelain can be identified sometimes by his name on the base, or his mark, the chemist's sign for tin (a figure 2 with a stroke through the horizontal baseline, like that of a figure 4). Queen's ware was marked by the royal arms and the words 'P.P.Coy L. (Plymouth Pottery Co Ltd) Stone China'. The one piece of blue and white in Plymouth City Museum believed to be from this pottery is not, however, marked.

The Coxside Gas Works of the Plymouth and Stonehouse Gas Co. were started in January 1846. Before the formation of the company a plant at

WORK ASHORE

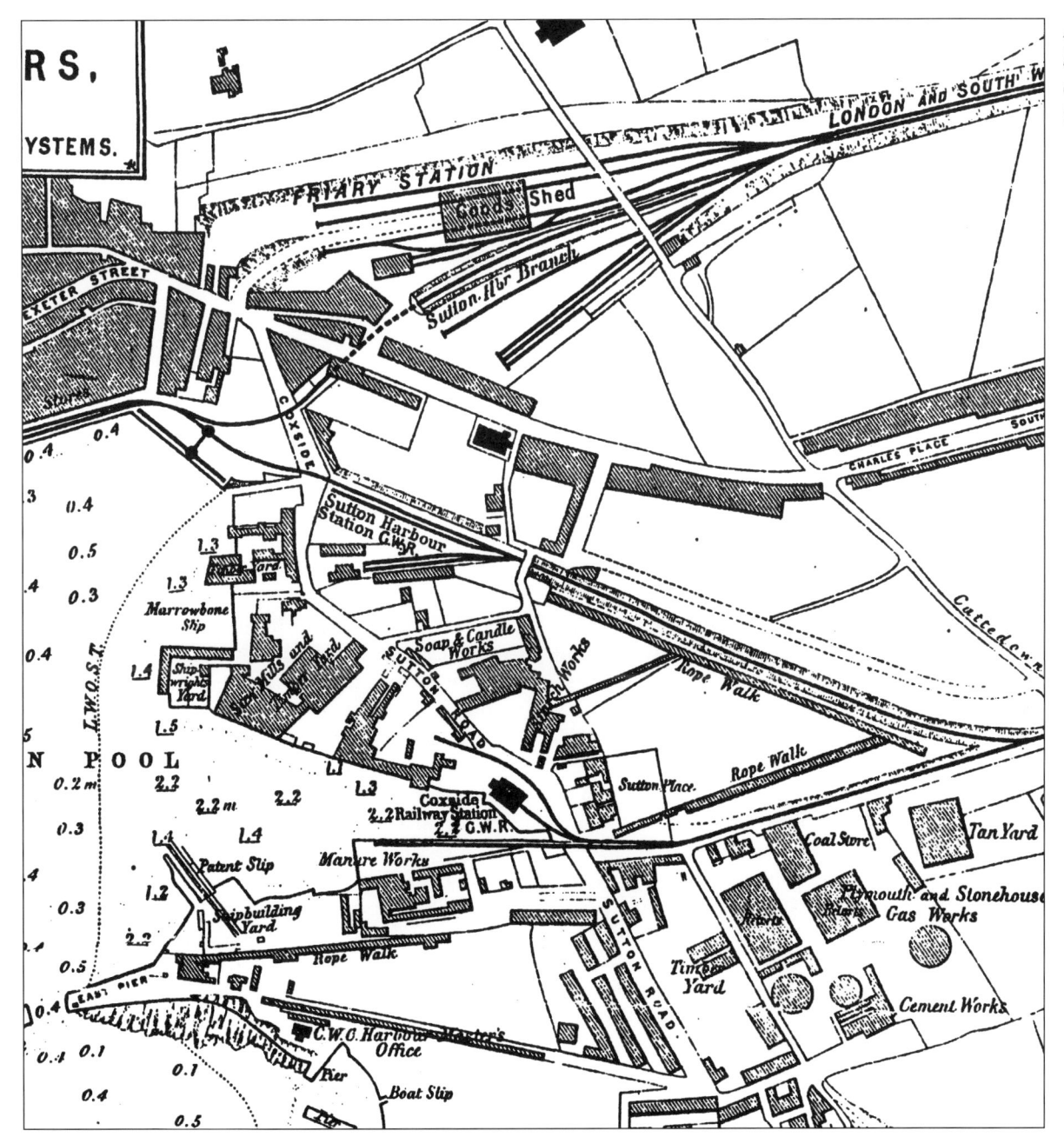

An 1879 plan of the harbour showing the congestion of factories in Coxside.

89

SUTTON HARBOUR

Opposite: An 1895 drawing of the New Patent Candle Company's factory in Sutton Road

Meeting House Slip and then Millbay, started in 1823, had supplied the town. That closed within two years of Coxside starting up. Its supplies were extended to Crownhill in 1904, to Plymstock in 1910, and in 1921 the Plympton area was taken over. At its peak the Coxside works occupied over 20 acres and employed nearly 250 men. Under nationalisation the South Western Gas Board took over in April 1948. Production of gas moved in 1966 to the Breakwater Quarry's new plant for making domestic gas from oil. This was soon supplanted by North Sea gas, and the gasholders at Coxside still store this natural gas. But the rest of the site has been cleared and empty for years.

Whether it was the by-products of gas, or a development from making linseed oil, varnish and tar products for shipping, or from sugar and salt refining; at any rate Plymouth turned to chemical and allied industries in the nineteenth century. A group of names are associated with this development and they range in and out of the different firms, switching partners. There is John Burnell, head of the South Devon Shipping Company, whose family had made tobacco pipes in Bretonside, William Bryant, Edward James, Francis May, Alger the potter, and Robert Burnard.

STARCH AND SUGAR

Bryant, James and May were all Quakers. In 1833 Bryant and James started sugar refining in Mill Lane, behind the present Methodist Central Hall, and Bryant also started a starch factory at the bottom of the lane, and later a candle works and the West of England Soap Company in Sutton Road. May joined them in experiments to make a match which would strike on sandpaper secured to the match-box. Hardly had they achieved success, developing the first match ever to strike on the box, than their factory burned down. James left the partnership but Bryant & May persevered, founding a factory to make matches in Bow, London. It still prospers, and the name of Bryant & May is still on every box of Swan Vestas.

In 1838 Burnell joined Bryant in the sugar refinery, and, five years later James began making starch in Sutton Road. He was later joined by Burnard and the business grew considerably, making washing blue, washing powders, soap powders and black lead. Edward James & Sons continued the business until 1905 when it passed into the hands of Reckitt & Sons Ltd (the proprietors were Quakers, like the Jameses) of Hull, who continued to make blue, black lead and Robin Starch, and did all the company printing, at the Sutton Road works until it was destroyed in the blitz of 1941.

In 1891 Mr J. Collier James recalled that his family lived in Clare House for some years after the factory was built, and recalled its four magnificent elms and a pink thorn tree, quite 40 ft across. In 1859 part of the house and the chapel was removed, and the rest of the house used as offices. His mother had told him stories of the poverty of the nuns who preceded them: the 'merry, chatty old lady' who was the Mother

Superior, and the story of the nun who eloped, being seen early one morning at the foot of Shepherd's Lane, wrapped in a cloak, where a gentleman met her in a carriage into which she stepped to be driven off rapidly. Between the time of the nuns and the James family, Clare House had been the home of Sir William Parker, 'the last of Nelson's captains'; this must clearly have been an impressive house and garden, hard to imagine today in Sutton Road.

One of the starch factory partners, Burnard, joined Alger in 1854 to launch a chemical works at Coxside. This later moved to Cattedown and was the foundation of that area's industrial development. It had already flowed along the eastern shore outside the harbour proper; Norrington was making artificial manure in Deadman's Bay, alongside Harvey's tar distillation plant.

Bryant and Burnell began to cut down their activities. In 1856 they sold their sugar refinery in Mill Lane to Sir Edward Bates, and in 1863 sold their West of England Soap Company in Sutton Road to the new Victoria Soap Company, alongside Thomas Gill's Millbay Soap Works. The Sutton Road plant was closed down. Thomas Gill still had Sutton Pool interests; in 1845 he was a partner with Derry and George Frean in a patent cement works on the north side of Coxside Creek. George Frean, an alderman of the council, had wide interests, ranging out to Dartmoor granite quarries - not surprising perhaps for the Johnson brothers were shipping their granite from the head of the creek and Derry had his copper ore yard on the south bank.

BISCUITS

When the Victualling Office at Lambhay had closed down, with the opening of the Royal William Yard at Stonehouse in 1830, Frean bought the bakery there and began to manufacture biscuits. He was joined by Daw and Serpell, who were flour millers at Drake's Mill, Sherwell. In 1857 Frean moved out, joining two Peek brothers, sons of a Kingsbridge man who had founded the great London firm of tea merchants, Peek Brothers. The Peek Frean fancy biscuit manufactory was started in Bermondsey. When the company was taken over by the American giant Nabisco in the 1980s, Peek Frean was the largest biscuit manufacturer in London. Of the Plymouth biscuit firm Robert Serpell in time became the only surviving partner and his son Henry transferred the whole concern to Reading, staff and all, in 1899. Reading still is an important biscuit-making centre and only recently have the names of Serpell and Peek Frean disappeared from biscuit tins.

The old storehouses between the bakery and West Pier, ranging along Commercial Wharf, had various uses. At one time they housed the Devon and Cornwall Manure Works; by the end of their days in the 1930s they were little more than boat stores; but fantastic, dark, low-ceilinged places they were. The widening of the road from the Barbican to Fisher's Nose, when the old fortifications were cut through to link up with Madeira Road, saw their end. Before that road was made pedestrians only could make the journey, climbing iron steps to go through a passage half tunnel, half-bridge covered with corrugated iron. The old stores between the bakery and the Emigration depot, Phoenix Wharf, were used for coal and grain.

Not until 1895 was Phoenix Wharf Pier opened to serve the red-funnelled steamers which Henry Elford had started in 1871, as the Oreston & Turnchapel Steamboat Company to bring people in from the villages across the Cattewater, and enable Plymouth people to go on jaunts to

SUTTON HARBOUR

A 1960s photograph of the tripper boats at Phoenix Wharf. A 'dockyard and warships' steamer is just leaving and another, in the foreground, is embarking passengers.

Jennycliffe and Bovisand. Many will remember the *Rapid, Lively, Swift* and *May Queen*, some even the earlier *Lady Beatrice*. The Elford family sold the company after the Second World War. Dinghy hards and the Mayflower Sailing Club, founded soon after the First World War, now occupy Phoenix and Baltic Wharfs, but in the tight industrial days of the nineteenth century there was even the Phoenix Chemical Works along the narrow strip that is now the head of the launching slip.

As the tightly-packed warehouses have opened out so fresh air has come to Sutton Harbour and the real beauty of its setting has become clear. The Barbican crowds now are tourists, not poor emigrants; the gift shops have taken over from the slop shops, and candle-lit restaurants have ousted the tiddleywinks. Artists and yachtsmen have replaced the topsail schoonermen and the hands from the Jersey packet boats.

It is a wealthier age than that of our grandfathers and Sutton Pool inevitably reflects it. But in few places can one be so close to the past; to the Victorian church-going industrialists of Coxside, the eighteenth-century merchants with their cargoes of sugar cane and tobacco; the short commons of the Siege and the exhilaration of Elizabethan days. Sutton Pool may never rank again as the sixth most important commercial harbour of Britain, but it is a natural harbour of too many advantages ever to be neglected.

CHAPTER 9
NEED FOR CHANGE

The bright picture presented by the Barbican and the surrounding streets began to look a little tarnished in the 1980s. In the harbour itself commercial trading, which had been dying for years, finally came to an end in May 1988 with the *Elaine W.* delivering the last cargo of coal. This end had long been anticipated, and the marina had deliberately been launched to replace the merchant shipping use of the harbour.

In the streets around, the revival of interest (initially created by the success of the Barbican Association and the improvement in the appearance of Southside Street, which early on had seen good antique shops and restaurants opening), began to go downmarket. People were still coming to the area but for the cheap gift shops and fast food outlets, the clubs and the pubs. There was a growing lager lout problem. The basic industry of the harbour, fishing, was stagnant if not declining.

BY-PASSING THE FISH MARKET

The boom years in fishing of the early 1970s had continued with varying returns for the rest of the decade, but in the early 1980s the returns only once passed the £3m mark, in 1982. In 1987 the total did reach £4m, and stayed close to this figure until a jump to over £5m in 1988. Until 1994 the total landings of fish in Plymouth were valued around the £4m mark. But both Newlyn and Brixham had shot well ahead, in 1994 Newlyn (dominated by the go-ahead Stevenson family) returned nearly £22m and Brixham (where the fishermen had formed a co-operative fish-selling operation in 1965, and the harbour authority responded by building a new market), nearly £15m. The Plymouth market was not even enjoying much of the business passing through the port. Of the £4.8m total for fish landed in 1994, only £0.8m was sold in the market. The Plymouth figures showed that shellfish (mainly scallops) totalled £2.1m, demersal £1.4m and pelagic £1.3m.

Scallops were not going through the market. Much of the pelagic (mackerel and pilchards) were being caught on contract and going straight into lorries on Bayly's Wharf and taken away for processing. Much fish was being landed at Cattedown Wharf for the new processing factory close behind the wharf. The factory, Interfish, was opened in 1985 by the Colam family, who had been long established in Manchester importing and exporting fish. In 1989 the brothers Jan and Frank built two new trawlers at a cost of £1m each. But these craft, the *Admiral Gordon* and the *Admiral Blake*, were operating for much of each year away from Plymouth, and landing their catch where the prices were best. When they did land at Plymouth their fish either went into the factory or was sent away to markets where better prices prevailed.

SUTTON HARBOUR

RESCUE OPERATIONS

The old cargo business had vanished, fishing was failing, the old industries had left Coxside (even gas-making had gone), and the streets were getting a bad name. Only the marina was flourishing, and the fishermen were grumbling that the harbour company was more concerned with yachties than with them. Fishermen like farmers are notorious grumblers; in fact the harbour company was already hard at work with plans for the future.

Its first concern after all was the fish market. Not only were market dues falling as it attracted less business, but so were landing charges. It was also becoming clear that new EC regulations would put the old 1890s fish market out of business. If a new one had to be built it wanted a new site.

On the other side of the harbour, land was lying idle. The coal transporters on Bayly's Wharf were still, the land unused. Lockyer's Quay was just being used to offload the mackerel catches. The gasworks at the head of the creek were idle. There was a low tide stretch of mud on its western side, behind East Pier. This could be reclaimed to give more shore space, as could the shallow head of Coxside Creek. A new fish market could be built there with an empty site all ready. The quay was owned by the harbour company but not the land behind, where a new fish market would have to be sited. Part belonged to Plymouth Coal Company, and the adjoining site to Calor Gas. It was not easy, and the negotiations with Calor Gas were long and protracted. But it was achieved. With bits of land behind the quay already owned by the company, and with judicious purchases, all the land backing the quays was eventually in the harbour company's hands.

In 1988 authority was obtained from Parliament to shift the fish market across the harbour. The Sea Fish Industry Authority, a powerful body financed jointly by the Government and the fishing industry, was commissioned to carry out a survey on the future of fishing in Plymouth. Their report was favourable.

LOCK GATES

If the market was to move, then more depth of water alongside the new fish quays would be welcome. As always when any major change was considered for the harbour, the old idea of lock gates came back to mind. Lock gates had first been mooted in 1786 and again in 1810-11. Detailed plans were made by Brunel in 1845, and the idea revived when the Barbican fish market was built in the 1890s. At that time there were still two men, Luscombe and Soltau, who had been on the board of the harbour company when it was floated in 1847. They remembered bitterly the Admiralty refusal of permission for lock gates two years before. In 1884, the year he retired as chairman of the company, William Luscombe, was complaining that thirty years of trade had been lost to Millbay because of the absence of lock gates to make Sutton a wet dock. The idea had never been forgotten.

There was also a new reason for building lock gates. Flooding of the area around the Parade and on Vauxhall Quay, particularly when low barometric pressure and south-westerly gales came on equinoctal spring tides, seemed to be happening more frequently and with less tolerance from the sufferers. The threatened global warming was expected to lift the level of high tides in the next fifty years. So lock gates could be presented to the National Rivers Authority, the national authority concerned with flood defences,

NEED FOR CHANGE

as a necessary safety measure. In the end the River Authority actually became the builders of the lock gates, with support from English Partnerships (the Government body founded and funded to help such projects), the City Council (because of the pedestrian access between the Barbican and Coxside) and the Sutton Harbour company.

Site investigations started in early 1990. It was found that both East and West Piers at the entrance to the harbour had sunk over the years, that there were internal voids of thirty per cent, and that the underlying limestone was highly fissured and fractured. All this meant that with lock gates closed the pressure of water pinned behind the walls at low water would produce an immense leakage, defeating the object of the gates.

So the first job was to make the piers and the underlying ground leakproof, as well as the ground on either side. A grouted curtain was formed right through both piers, and through the rock beneath to a depth of forty-five metres below low tide level. The curtain extended thirty metres up Castle Street as well as under Bayly's and Lockyer's Wharfs. The shafts in the piers were turned into concrete columns as a precaution against future sinking. All this work cost £750 000, nearly a quarter of the total contract, and at the end there was nothing on the surface to show for it!

After various debates on how the lock gates were to be built the final consulting engineers were L.G.Mouchel and the builders Christiani & Neilson. The contract, for £4.2m, started on 1 January 1992. Quarrying was opened in the old Teat's Hill Quarry, behind the former coal stores and old warehouses on Bayly's Wharf, a crusher installed, and the stone used first of all to build a coffer dam across the top of Coxside Creek. The dam was made waterproof and the sea bed behind levelled. On this the whole structure of the dam was built as one unit, in reinforced concrete, base, sides and all, 66m long, 33m wide and 10.25m high. In all it weighed 9000 tonnes.

Around the southern end of Bayly's Wharf concrete foundations were laid underwater. On shore the quay wall was being built. This consisted of a series of reinforced concrete units of varying size, weighing between 47 and 54 tonnes. When all was ready they were lowered into position, one after another. The 500-ton mobile crane used was only one of two in the country capable of handling such weights; it had to be hired from Manchester and work stopped from time to time when it was needed elsewhere.

The final position of the lock gates was partly over the end of the east pier, which had to be demolished to make way. Alongside the lock a second entrance had to be constructed, for use in

The 'bund' across the top of Coxside Creek which provided dry ground on which to build the lock.

SUTTON HARBOUR

Top left: *The lock under construction, showing the large cavities which enabled the lock to be floated into position.* Top right: *The walls for the new quay being built, seen from behind. Each section of wall has a supporting flange at the back.* Lower left: *The quay wall sections in position, continuing the line of Bayly's Wharf.* Lower right: *The lock is towed into its final position.*

emergencies such as the lock machinery failing. It would be closed by what were called stoplogs, actually made of metal. The idea was based on the 'bock' gates of the little Cornish fishing harbours where, in bad storms, lengths of timber are lowered by a crane into slots on either side of the harbour entrance, one on top of another, to make temporary gates. So they block the waves from disturbing the harbour and the moored craft, and the word 'bock' has passed into West Country dialect, meaning 'to get in the way'.

When the lock was finished, and before it could be put into place its final bed had to be meticulously levelled to take the concrete base. Once that was done the dam, all 9000 tonnes, had to be floated around to its final resting place. There was empty cells in the walls which would help it to float, and the stoplogs, the 'bocks', were borrowed to fill in the ends of the lock. The temporary coffer dam was removed, two big tugs were hired from the dockyard, and just before high-water springs on 23 April 1993, some hours before dawn, the whole 9000 tonnes of the lock floated and the tow began.

The first heave of the tugs pulled the foot of the front end down and the structure stuck. But before high water was reached it came afloat again, and very, very gingerly the whole operation was completed, the lock towed out of Coxside Creek, turned through ninety degrees, coaxed into position and sunk in its final bed. The sun was up when all was done, and the spectators on the quaysides were nearly as relieved as the engineers and the seamen themselves.

The air cavities in the lock walls were filled with sand to act as ballast. The whole had been designed so that West Pier was left intact, with a structure built on the end to take the stoplogs, with a similar slot on the side of the dam opposite.

Inside the lock basin, preparing for the lock gates to be installed.

While the final work was being done on the lock the temporary entrance was used. The pre-constructed lock gates were put in place, the control point built on the edge and the computer-operated controls put into position. The swing bridge for pedestrian use across the harbour entrance was set up. All this mechanical and electrical work was the subject of a separate £1m contract. The 'bocks' were removed and placed to close the emergency opening.

The gates are kept open from half flood tide to half ebb, so that for three hours either side of high water the tide flows in and out, to maintain water quality in the harbour. The water level is never less than four metres above low tide level. It only takes a minute to open the bridge during the high water period, and it takes a vessel between two and ten minutes, depending on the state of the tide, to pass through the lock. The navigable width of the gates is 12 metres.

SUTTON HARBOUR

The massive lock gates in position.

A fuel pay terminal, catering for all nationalities.

THE FISH MARKET

Once the lock gates had been floated out a wall was built across Coxside Creek, between Lockyer's and Johnson's quays, enclosing another 5000 square metres. On the reclaimed land at the end of Bayly's Wharf the new fish market was built, at a cost of £3m. The building was designed by the Architects Design Group of Plymouth and erected by MacAlpines. It is on a north-south line, with doors opening on to the west-facing quay through which incoming fish can be landed, and more doors on the landward side through which the sold fish can be loaded into lorries for dispatch. At the north end is free chiller storage where fish landed overnight can await the auction. Free sorting and grading with electronic scales is available. A long glass-fronted gallery looks down on the market floor. The gallery opens on the other side to suites of offices where, among others, are lodged the Ministry of Agriculture and Fish's offices of the district fisheries inspector, the market company, and the office of the new National Marine Aquarium. On the roof is an ice-making plant capable of holding 80 tonnes of ice which can be supplied at any time direct to a fishing boat alongside. There is also a 24-hour fuel supply service, either automatic or manned, available from three points on the quayside.

Behind the market proper, running at right angles to the market building, offices and work areas for the merchants were built. Behind the offices is a high-speed box wash, and a block of lock-up stores for the fishermen. There was ample car parking space. A new road was built by the highway authority linking the new market with the main road system out of Plymouth, so that this road and A38 provided a four-lane carriageway all the way to the national motorway system.

THE HARBOUR COMPANY

All these developments were not happening neatly spaced out, to be dealt with one at a time. They were all interlocking. One depended on another; they were all urgent, and all enormously expensive. The 1847 structure of the Improvement Company, even with various changes made over the years, was not going to be able to cope with the new ambitions of the directors, and the flexibility to develop. The old company for instance could only use harbour land for harbour purposes. All this produced five years plus of probably the most hectic time in the company's history.

The main burden fell on the managing director, Duncan Godefroy (a Huguenot name). He had joined the company in 1962, at the age of 22, as secretary. Brought up in Plymouth, he had worked previously in acountancy and in transport. Now he had to call into play his basic skills

NEED FOR CHANGE

as well as his thirty-five years experience with the company. He was actively supported by his chairman, Brian Foster, a stockbroker, and by the deputy chairman, Peter Stedman. A surveyor who had originally been advising the company on property matters, Peter had been invited to become a director in 1966. By the time of these developments he and Duncan, who had joined the Board a few months earlier, were the oldest serving directors.

When the company was first formed, and for many years after, its directors had been men whose business depended on the harbour, and so the company was administered, understandably, to benefit their principal interests rather than simply as a money-making company. It had always kept in profit, but fundamentally it had always been run for the benefit of the harbour. Now its directors were not directly concerned, except as shareholders, with the harbour. But in the main they were Plymothians, and continued to run the company not primarily to make a profit, but for the greater good of the harbour and the city.

NEW COMPANIES

The old company was severely limited in what it could do, by the Act of Parliament under which it was formed. This needed changing, but to go for a private Act of Parliament was expensive, and chancy. So in 1989 a 'scheme of arrangement' was obtained from the High Court under which all the shares of the Sutton Harbour Improvement Company could be transferred to Sutton Harbour Holdings Ltd, which in time became Sutton Harbour Holdings plc and the sole owner of the harbour.

In the same year, the holding company set up a number of subsidiary companies. Eventually Sutton Harbour Fisheries Ltd became Plymouth Fisheries and provided fishing facilties. Sutton Harbour Services Ltd provided engineering and boat repair services for both fishing and yachting. Sutton Harbour Developments Ltd was responsible for the management of the properties as well as investors and developers (Peter Stedman naturally became chairman of this subsidiary).

To fund all these new developments Sutton Harbour Holdings plc made a new issue of five million £1 shares at par in August 1996. Applications received were well in excess when the offer closed, and shares were immediately at a premium, being quoted at £1.20. One of the biggest investors was Rotolox (Holdings) Ltd whose chairman was Dan McCauley, better known locally as chairman of Plymouth Argyle and owner of Drake's Island. By October he owned about 15 per cent of the company.

OPERATING THE MARKET

Inevitably the building of a new market for a fishing industry faced with so many restrictions in what it could catch, with the inevitable higher

The first merchant's offices, with the new fish market in the background

Sutton Harbour Master, Pat Marshall (left), with the company's Contract Manager, Martin Emden.

charges which came with modernisation, in a port where the industry was in apparent decline, produced many doubts. There was considerable scepticism about the viability of the new market. The Sutton Harbour company itself designed a market building which (just in case) could be turned to other uses. The old merchants were not sure they could pay the new charges. In the old market one merchant had done all the auctioneering, and the fishermen were not happy with the system.

So Duncan Godefroy persuaded the fishermen to form their own agency which would run the market, of which they were given the sole use (they only pay rent for their office), and conduct all auctions. The harbour company helped financially, and guaranteed the overdraft of the new agency. The articles of the new company, Plymouth Trawler Agents Ltd, laid down that 75 per cent of the shares were to be held by fishermen or members of the fishing community. In the event 98 per cent are so held, in keeping with the intention of the founders that power in the company should be kept in the fishing fraternity. The first directors, David Pessell, Ray Parsons, Graham Andrews and Ken Parry, were all local inshore trawler owners, and David Pessell, elected chairman, had been a leader of Plymouth fishermen for a number of years. They are all unpaid, and do not draw any expenses. Peter Bromley, a local trawlerman, was appointed as the harbour company's manager of the fish market, and the Agency appointed 36-year-old Shaun Lyth, of an old Whitby fishing family, as its manager, auctioneer and sole agent.

Control of the Plymouth market thus passed effectively from the merchants, who had held it for decades, to the fishermen. A rival fish market was set up in nearby premises, which had been Rowe Brothers fruit market, and some people scared by the rents in the new market began to use it. But with a few months this competing market had collapsed.

RECOVERY

The new Plymouth fish market opened in February 1995. In that year the total Plymouth returns leapt to £6.5m. Of this total, £2.1m passed through the market. In 1996, the first full year of operating the new market, the final figure for the port was over £11m and the new market contributed £7m to this figure; a considerable change from the £0.8m of the last year on the old site!

Before the new market had been finished a big national firm, Rossfish Ltd, rented three of the office spaces. They regularly buy in the market and process and pack fish in their units. Much of the fish sold by Tesco is bought from Rossfish, and the central distribution centre which serves the other main supermarkets is expected to buy more in Plymouth. Other national fish-buying companies have since moved in, and all the units are occupied, some by local wholesalers like Rex Down and S.& J. who have moved across the harbour with the market. Another is occupied by Underwood Shellfish which processes crabs and the like, and whose business has multiplied considerably with the move from their old New Street warehouse. Also established in a unit is Plymouth Fisheries Chandlery Services, which provides a full trawl-making and wire-splicing service, as well as providing an extensive range of fishing equipment.

Where in the old market there were six or seven buyers, now there are fifty to sixty. Prices were improving. More boats were landing, with big trawlers from Scotland (up to twenty visiting boats at any one time), Portsmouth and other ports moving their operations to Plymouth.

NEED FOR CHANGE

Belgian and Scottish vessels began landing large catches of cuttlefish and bass, which had previously been landed in France. The first bulk supplies for many years of tuna, hake and megrim were also coming in.

Interfish's new trawlers, and the *Gillian E*, another big rebuilt Plymouth trawler which had also been operating away from Plymouth, were now landing more and more for the new market. When the *Admiral Gordon* and *Admiral Blake* were landing at Padstow, they sent their catches by road to Plymouth market. Plymouth craft which had been landing their catches at Brixham and Newlyn for better prices, were now using their home market. Stern trawlers from other ports, such as Looe, Polperro, Mevagissey, Padstow, Bideford, Ilfracombe and the Isle of Man, were also using Plymouth, for the better prices. In the first twenty months of the new market, 226 different craft had been landing their catches.

Between the opening of the new market and the end of 1996 the largest catch to come to the market fetched £39,000. Two Scottish trawlers, working as a pair and fishing for bass, landed a catch that grossed £160,000 from one eight-day voyage. The best catch of bass, a high-value fish, was twenty-three tonnes from one shot of the trawl. Other prime species, such as dover sole and turbot, were regularly fetching over £80 a stone. In the spring of 1997 three or four big Zeebrugge trawlers were landing regularly. In one week in March £400,000 of fish was landed, £300,000 of which passed through the market. In the old market only £800,000 of business was handled in the whole year.

In the winter of 1996-7 the Plymouth fleet of big craft comprised the two *Admirals*, the *Gillian E* (which had been sold to a Scottish company but was still manned locally), four Jersey owned and registered craft (*Pieter J, Evert Maryte, Pieter and Grietje*) which were manned by Pymouth men and based in the port, and the Teignmouth registered *Niblick* also owned and manned in Plymouth. Between thirty and forty under-10 metre craft, which do not have a quota and so are more free, make up the local fleet. Apart from the quota (and the mackerel box off Plymouth in which none of these fish can be caught, set up to preserve the overfished area), the Government is also trying to reduce the fleet. They were paying owners to break up their craft and leave the industry. Seven old Plymouth boats were decommissioned under this scheme, six of them scallopers. But under a loophole in the law, six of these owners were building new, modern, more powerful white-fish vessels. So the fleet based in Plymouth is actually increasing.

The number of people employed by the industry in the port varies with the season, but the full-time fishermen total about 260, the market staff 20, the various drivers, salesmen, clerks and those engaged in cleaning and handling fish, another 120. That adds up to 400, with another 100 at Interfish, making a total of 500 plus.

Big trawlers in the harbour, moored five-abreast

SUTTON HARBOUR

THE MARINA

The boom years of the Thatcher era did bring growth in the luxury trades. People had money to spend on yachts, and as the dinghy enthusiasts of the postwar period got older and needed more comfort, so did the market grow for yachts, and yacht berths.

Sutton Harbour marina, with 200 berths in 1974, had a waiting list of another 200 by 1975. By the early 1980s more pontoons had increased the berths to 300. In 1994 this was reduced to 275 to allow larger yachts to be berthed. There is still a waiting list. A number of berths are kept for visiting yachtsmen, who can call the marina office by radio to make a booking as they approach the port.

In the berths fresh water is available, and mains electricity connections. Fuel, lubricants and gas supplies are available from a pontoon close to the marina office. Each berth has a car parking space on the quayside,

With the extension southwards of the pontoons the office was moved in 1989 from the first floor of the building in the corner between Sutton Wharf and North Quay, which was then rented to a firm of architects. The ablutions remained on the ground floor of this block, but a new office was built on top of the single-storey offices on Sutton Jetty, at the seaward end. This was right above the berths for visiting yachtsmen, and was better placed for a watch on all yachts. Local boatmen who do not want the expensive facilities of the marina still have moorings off North and North-East Quays, and on old pontoons moored off Harbour Marine.

In addition to the yachts using the marina, two research vessels of the Marine Biological Association's laboratory on the Hoe are also based on the pontoons.

HARBOUR MARINE

In the 1970s the waterside behind the Shipwright's Arms, in Sutton Road, was a tangle of old disused warehouses with a high wall running along the water's edge. On an empty piece of land behind the wall Michael Willow, a boat builder by trade, opened a boatyard in 1981. He had to crane the boats over the wall and had very little space, but he could offer repair work and some boat storage. He started with one man working with him, and his wife coming in her spare time from a city centre office to do the books.

When the Sutton Harbour company, which owned the area, began clearing the wall and the old buildings, Harbour Marine moved to a small store at the back of Marrowbone Slip beach. With the clearance complete, the harbour company built the Sugar House in 1985, and recovered some the land in front, building a new sea wall and a slipway. Mike rented some of the workshop space on the ground floor and resumed his activity on the cleared area in front. Harbour Marine prospered, more staff were taken on, and Irene Willow had to give up her day job to become full-time office manager. Growth in fact overtook the Willows to such an extent that in 1993 they approached the Sutton Harbour company, who made a very friendly take-over, with Mr and Mrs Willow remaining to run the business. That year marine engineering was added to the skills on offer

Subsequently Sutton Harbour Services Ltd took over Stainless Steel Services, who manufactured components in a workshop adjoining Harbour Marine, and made it part of Harbour Marine. Now the repair facilities of the yard are offered to both marina and the fishing complex. At the end of 1996 Harbour Marine had a fifteen-ton mobile crane and a total workforce of twelve. They can store fifty boats up to 40ft in length.

To add to the facilities the harbour offered, the fisheries company also opened a fishing chandlery in the new market area.

EXPANDED HOUSING

The Barbican Asociation had converted a warehouse at the bottom of New Street into very successful flats, and other people took up the idea. A warehouse on Vauxhall Quay was converted (one early tenant was Jim Woodrow, chairman of both the Barbican Association and Sutton Harbour Improvement Company, and his wife). Around the corner on Sutton Quay the old fruit and vegetable warehouse which had housed the French onion sellers in its time, became in 1983 another complex called Dolphin Court, with shops on the ground floor, offices on the first floor and eighteen flats above that.

In 1985 a warehouse on North Quay and the derelict wine stores of the Hawker firm, by now out of business, were bought by a developer. He rebuilt the wine store, on the corner of Hawker's Avenue, to match the existing warehouse, using limestone blocks from the Royal Albert Hospital at Devonport, which was being demolished at that time, as facing. The joint building, called Harbourside Court, produced 52 flats.

Various other small flat developments took place in and around Southside Street, and on Quay Road. The City Council abandoned its policy of stopping people living over the shops in Southside Street, and even allowed it on top floors of Barbican Association houses in New Street. At the top of New Street a national housing association built Hanover House in 1969, twenty flats of sheltered accomodation, with a stepped frontage to give the residents a view down the street. Below the Robin Hood club the Tamar Housing Society built more flats in 1967, which they called John Sparke House.

More flats came on North Quay in 1989. Developers acquired the derelict warehouses west of Harbour Avenue, cleared the site, and applied for permission to erect an eleven-storey block of flats. A horrified Planning Committee cut them down, but still allowed a block of seven storeys on the quayside, and even higher behind, both too tall for their neighbours, and allowed a white stucco finish under the gabled roofline. Mariner's Court, as this complex is called, houses in all four shops, four mews houses and 78 flats.

At the other end of North Quay the Co-op warehouse rebuilt after the Second World War was knocked down in 1990 and it was planned to erect another block of offices topped by flats. But the developers went bankrupt. In 1995 the part-built block was bought by Michael Antonucci, the descendant of a group of Italian emigrants from a village near Naples who, in the 1880s, had set off for the United States but got no further than Plymouth. The Antonuccis settled in Bretonside, selling ice cream and later fish and chips. Michael was running an antiques business from the family shop in Bretonside when he won nearly £3m in the lottery. He bought the Salvation Army halls next door when they moved out in 1996, and turned them into an auction gallery and a tea shop. He initially used the old Co-op site as a car park.

BROCK HOUSE

Two leading members of the City Council, Ernest and Cissie Brock, are remembered in Brock House, sheltered housing built in 1992 at the bottom of Batter Street. The Brock Trust was set up and the funds provided by the wills of the two

SUTTON HARBOUR

The tower of Castle Street School in its schooldays. It is now retained as a feature of a block of flats.

Brocks paid for the flats built jointly by the Trust and the City Council. It is on the site of the former Mayoralty House, and was the subject of a revealing archaeological investigation which tied up with work already done on the other side of Vauxhall Street. The long history of the site is depicted in mosaic murals in the Batter Street entrance, with more wall panels in the hall inside A listed warehouse at the top of New Street, which had been the wine store of Colliers, whose offices in Southside Street had become the print shop of William Fox-Smith, was taken over by the Sovereign Housing Association. In 1997, with the help of £200,000 from English Partnerships, they started converting the stores into twenty-six units of sheltered accomodation.

The Corporation has also refurbished most of its blocks of flats in the Sutton Harbour area, and virtually rebuilt the interior of its early council house developments in Looe Street and How Street. So the area now has living side-by-side the council house dwellers - many of whom have bought their flats and houses from the Council - and the middle class flat dwellers in the new blocks.

In spite of this new housing the population declined in numbers. As the people who moved into the 1930s council developments became older, so the numbers of children fell. The elementary schools closed; Castle Street, Palace Court, Treville Street (for some years a secondary modern), Sutton Road, Cattedown Road. The education authority found new uses for most of them, but Castle Street was replaced by more middle-class flats with the tower kept as an architectural feature. The Seamen's Bethel and mission churches like Lower Street and Clare, vanished. Religion was served by St Andrew's and St John-Sutton-on-Plym for the Anglicans, Holy Cross for the Catholics, and Catherine Street for the Baptists. Holy Cross kept its primary school, the only one reasonably close to the harbour area. St Andrew's School was destroyed in the war and rebuilt on the site of St James-the-Less, another wartime casualty and a long way from the Barbican. There was for a time a charismatic church in a New Street warehouse, Palace Court, but that too vanished when the developers of Mariner's Court obtained planning permission to convert that into flats.

CHANGING SCENE

The increasing standard of living which had led to yachts replacing dinghies, lifted the standard of council housing and brought new residents into the area, wrought other changes. The old village shops went from Southside Street and Bretonside, as they were vanishing in every other suburb in the country. The ship chandlers, instrument makers and others who had serviced the seafaring side of life, disappeared. In their place came antique shops, art galleries, restaurants and gift shops. Plymouth people came shopping here as they never had before, and visitors were attracted as much by the new shops as by the historic background.

As always seems to happen with tourism, the cheap drove out the best. Gradually the antique shops gave way to more and more gift shops, and fast food outlets rivalled the fish and chips. The post office became a fish and chip shop. The pharmacy vanished. Clubs which were near-pubs sprouted; many of the pubs themselves changed character. Under new licensing laws the closing time came later and later. Southside Street and the Parade became a night-time alternative to Union Street. The place acquired an unsavoury reputation. Appeals were made to the City Council: 'they' should do something about it.

CHAPTER 10
BRIGHT NEW WORLD

In the 1980s Plymouth and its planners were looking hard at the whole of the city's waterfront. From the South Yard of Devonport Dockyard right around to Laira Bridge there were sites abandoned by industry, run down by neglect. A series of expensive publications, studded with colour pictures, began to appear. *West Coast Watershed; Planning for Plymouth into the 1990s* came from the Planning Department in 1989 and that same year a report commissioned from private consultants was published. The following year a 'Strategy' appeared. The Civic Trust was invited to prepare plans for Sutton Harbour and the Barbican. They published a consultation document in 1990, and a final report in 1992. Plymouth Development Corporation took over Mount Wise, the Royal William Yard and Mount Batten from the Ministry of Defence and began publishing glossy annual reports and sales brochures. Year after year the brighly coloured brochures and booklets appeared, till the number ran into double figures.

Work did begin in the Sutton Harbour area. The highway authority, Devon County Council, built a new road christened Hoe Approach from Notte Street to Citadel Road, intended to carry traffic away from Southside Street. This was pedestrianised with wider pavements and single lane roadway. In common with other neighbouring streets it was expensively repaved with limestone, but as the local stone was no longer available Italian stone was used, rather brighter that the local. Quay Road, the property of the harbour company, was closed to traffic. But road users paid little attention to the banning of traffic from Southside Street, and after a time the pedestrianation was quietly forgotten.

New signs were commissioned by Plymouth City Council to mark the entrances to the Barbican, with the biggest and best on Mayflower Pier. This represented a mythological fish on a pole, aroused much ironic laughter and was christened the 'Barbican Prawn'. But it stayed

Traffic chaos in Southside Street in the days before cars were restricted.

SUTTON HARBOUR

A 'dig' in progress: Archaeologists excavate the merchants' houses and warehouses on North Quay, now the car park of North Quay House. The inlet of water beside Hawker's Avenue shows how these developments were pushed out into the harbour.

put, and began to be accepted as quietly amusing. Hardly were the pavements laid before Eurobell lifted them all to instal cable television.

The planning was paying off. At a meeting at the end of 1996 it was said that more than £24m had been injected into the area in all, in the last few years. At this meeting the Council was launching another £7m regeneration scheme, mainly funded by the Government's Single Regeneration Fund and the European Regional Development Fund. Its aims were to improve the environment, the facilities for tourism and business development.

THE ARCHAEOLOGISTS

There was also a growing interest in the past. Between 1963 and 1969 the late James Barber and a team recruited by the City Museum were able to investigate the area between Vauxhall Street and the Parade now occupied by council flats. It was one of the first excavations of a waterfront site anywhere in Britain, and revealed evidence for development from about 1250.

In 1990 a further excavation by an Exeter Museum team on the other side of Vauxhall Street, a site now occupied by Brock House, revealed a sequence of construction from at least the fourteenth century. The original dwelling houses and warehouses were built at right angles to the shore with space between them for ships to be docked. In the fullness of time sea walls were built out beyond these houses to make a continuous quay.

Planning guidance issued that year put the onus of archaeological investigation of any site on the developer: it has been expensive for developers but has yielded famous results for the historian. Such an investigation in 1994-5 on the site of North Quay House showed the extensive reclamation of the foreshore in 1649-50. Evidence of merchants' houses, warehouses, slipways and cobbled lanes was recorded and then preserved beneath the present car park and building. Then digs on Dung Quay showed a series of quay walls being built out into the harbour over the centuries, and other work in the China House and on Shepherd's Wharf revealed more of the early Commonwealth quayside investments, when the authority of the Prince of Wales over the harbour had been abolished.

Dr Keith Ray, the city archaeological officer, has neatly summarised all this work in a paper, 'Sutton-super Plymouth: a Medieval Port' in *Plymouth Archaeology*, No 2 published in 1995. Archaeologists were also busy during the building of the lock gates, assessing the piers, quay walls and foreshore all round the harbour; aware that only in exceptional circumstances would the tide ever fall below the half tide mark again.

SEWAGE TREATMENT

In 1995, as the City Council was improving the pavements around Sutton Harbour, South West Water embarked on a major sewage treatment scheme for central Plymouth. Instead of the raw sewage being poured into the sea at Fisher's Nose, it was all to be piped to a new plant at Prince Rock and then piped back, as pure as could be, to be dispersed from the old Fisher's Nose outlet. Fortunately they built large deep tunnels to carry all the piping, which only needed various shafts as access points. In 1996 one shaft was dug in the triangle on the Parade (lifting temporarily the new paving, but yielding interesting archaeological finds). Another shaft was sunk in the small car park opposite Bretonside bus station. As a result the old sewage storage tanks under the Parade and the Barbican fish market became simply part of the pipe system carrying the sewage.

CAR PARKING

For many years car parking in the area has been a problem. With parking gone from Southside Street and Quay Road, and the harbour company closing off the area it owned on the Barbican (the 1895 extension) at the request of the City Council, the problem became acute. Much earlier a plan had been put forward for a large car park at the top of Hoegate Street, partly cutting into the Hoe. This would have helped enormously, but some residents in Frobisher Terrace called in the Royal Fine Arts Commission. They decided it would ruin the view of the Citadel, and banned the idea.

By this time plans were well advanced for the new fish market on Bayly's Wharf, and a new national marine aquarium on the Deadman's Bay foreshore of Teat's Hill. So Devon County built a car park on Lockyer's Quay which would serve both fish market and aquarium. By using the footpath over the lock at the entrance to the harbour the car park could also be used by visitors to the western side of the harbour. It was christened the Barbican Car Park, although quite a distance from the Barbican, let alone the shops of Southside Street. The new fish market had its own car park, the aquarium had yet to be built, and the much vaunted multi-storey car park, opened in April 1995, was largely left empty.

BOAT TRIPS

Visiting coaches still rumbled through Southside Street to drop their passengers at Mayflower Pier or Phoenix Wharf where ready-chartered pleasure boats were waiting. During the summer, a season which seems to start earlier and finish later each year, the cruisers are busy serving tourists by day and local groups in the evenings. The old familiar 'Four rivers and Dockyard', or 'Dockyard and Warships' is still popular, with longer trips up the Tamar to Calstock and, once or twice a season, to Weir Head, or else out to the Yealm and Cawsand.

The biggest company, Plymouth Boat Cruises, works from Phoenix Wharf. It was created in 1982 and took over the boats of the old Millbrook Steam Company in 1985; the fleet includes the *Plymouth Venturer, Plymouth Princess, Totnes Castle, Southern Belle, Western Belle* and the smaller *Weston Maid* which runs a summer ferry service to Cawsand from the Mayflower Steps. The other company, Tamar Cruising, operates the *Plymouth Sound* from the Mayflower Steps.

THE STREETS

In spite of all the problems, life began to improve. A food and wine supermarket opened in Southside Street, in what had been Andrade's antique shop, and flourished. Good quality restaurants like La Bella Napoli, started in 1966, and Piermasters, survived. This latter had an interesting background; for over two hundred years the Hannam family had fed fishermen there and served them with cups of tea. Mrs E.J.Hannam eventually retired in the 1960s at the age of 89. and afer varous vissicitudes the premises were opened by a company in 1979. Stephen Williams became chef and then manager in 1984, and while Piermasters still specialises in fish it has now a rather different clientele.

The quality of the gift shops improved. Anthony and Dorothy Clements, who opened their second-hand bookshop in Southside Street in 1966, made the most of their business although they crossed the road to a smaller shop in 1996.

Feeding the fishermen back in the 1960s. Mrs Elizabeth Hannam at her old black coal stove. This has now been replaced by the modern kitchens of Piermasters restaurant.

SUTTON HARBOUR

Of the other arrivals of the post Second World War vintage, Chris Robinson has been selling prints of his own drawings of the area in an Elizabethan building in New Street since 1984; he had started higher up the street in 1978. William Fox-Smith with his antique engravings and maps in Southside Street not only came through the dark days around 1990, but doubled the size of his shop. William Hodges in the Barbican Gallery on the Parade was another successful survivor, and in 1995 his son opened another gallery, called Barbican Gallery Too, in Southside Street. Sonia Donovan in the Armada Gallery, tucked away in Parade Ope, weathered the storm, and even opened two more galleries, going upmarket in Southside Street. Her former upstairs gallery became a showplace for Robert Lenkiewicz's remarkable paintings, with a new approach through a downstairs gallery created in a shop on the corner of the Parade.

Tope's sail-making business had disappeared, as had the shellfish dressing place on the ground floor in Citadel Ope. Shops had replaced them both, with offices over the top. Next door the James L. Nash fruit and vegetable warehouse had folded and Jack Nash, grandson of the founder, converted the building in 1982 into 'The House that Jack Built', with narrow arcades and staircases winding through eighteen small shops. Over the years the little shops had been joined together into ten larger ones.

OLDEST INHABITANTS

There are three survivals. At the bottom of Southside Street is Jacka's Bakery; its oven is the base of an Elizabethan chimney-stack, which suggests that it has been a bakery for centuries. It has always been a family business. The Fomes had it in the nineteenth century until a daughter married a Warren and it became Fome & Warren, and then Warren. Frederick Jacka bought the business in the 1930s, his nephew, Hugh Jacka took over in 1952, and sold it to the present baker, Roger Compton, in 1986.

Another business, now in fourth-generation hands at least, is that of C.R.Cload, the chandlers on the Barbican. The family started in Exchange Street, again in the nineteenth century, and in 1905 the then Charlie Cload (the eldest son is always C.R.) bought the Barbican shop from Dunstans, the ship chandlers, who moved into Southside Street. In the 1930s when Alderman Lovell Dunstan was leader of the Conservative Party and the dominant figure in the Council, C.R.Cload was the councillor for the Vintry Ward. The first Cload on the Barbican was in the early days of engines and the premises were virtually an engine supply point and repair base. Over the years as needs changed, so they became fishing chandlers; nowadays they cater more for yachtsmen. Colin Cload took over the business in 1995, when his elder brother, another Charlie, retired.

What must be the oldest one-family shop in the street, the Yarmouth Stores, was first opened in

The Yarmouth Stores in Southside Street, owned by the same family for over a century, and little changed.

1898. It has always been in the hands of the Knights, a Yarmouth family, and in 1997 the owner, Christopher Knight, was still living there. It opened as a fishermen's outfitter's, and in 1997, approaching its century and with the shop assistant, Mrs G.Paterson, with twenty-eight years service in the shop, it looked as if it has never changed . But it has served a much wider clientele in its later years, and its gear appeals now not just to yachtsmen and fishermen, but also to the fashion conscious who have no links with the sea.

THE CHANGING SCENE

As the 1990s marched on, the shops in Southside Street improved in quality, so that by day the area became a pleasant place for browsing shoppers. In high summer it can be rather crowded with visitors, but the crowds are amiable. Nighttime, particularly at weekends, the crowds are pub crawling; it is a lively place humming with vitality; often noisy and boisterous but rarely offensive. The pubs themselves, the Council and the police, are all doing their best to keep it that way. Wandering from pub to pub with glass and bottles in hand is not allowed, but by day a number of pubs and tea shops are allowed outside seating in the sun. The Parade and the car-free Quay Road have the space to encourage this.

By 1997 the whole scene, from one side of the harbour to the other, had changed dramatically from what it was even after peace in 1946. By 1990, for example, the Citadel had rid itself of all the tatty and little-used sheds and military debris on the slopes of Lambhay Hill, and built a high limestone wall which in time will look as old as the original walls of 1660. Behind this was created parking space and garages for the multitude of motor vehicles needed by the modern military.

As one walks back towards the harbour the lock gates and the new fish market dominate the scene. West Pier, alias the Mayflower Pier, has only changed to take the swing bridge at the end, but the cobbling and the pavements are improved. The seats are specially-designed overgrown cleats with metal plates on top engraved with Chris Robinson drawings and historical notes to explain to visitors what they can see around them.

On the Barbican the high railway station canopy that roofed the fish market from 1896 to 1994 had been cleansed of all the white-tiled offices, and with glass walls houses a new Dartington Hall glass factory and shop, and a demonstration area. At the south end a new strange-shaped kiln was opened in 1997, which pushed Cap'n Jasper's snack bar out of its accustomed place; he now operates from the old police station on White House Pier. John Dudley, who

Tony Jago, a Cawsand fisherman, stands with a cup of tea outside Cap'n Jasper's, with a Lenkiewicz painting of Cap'n Jasper (John Dudley) on the door.

SUTTON HARBOUR

started Cap'n Jasper's in 1978, has achieved a world-wide reputation as an up-market snack bar. Before 1978 he had a wine and seafood bar in Southside Street, having started in the business with the well-reputed Dudley's Brewhouse in Kingsbridge.

RAILINGS

This side of the harbour no longer has a working quay. From Mayflower Pier around to the start of North Quay the water's edge is lined with railings like a seaside promenade - which is what the old fish quay and the rest have become. The working fish quay is now across the harbour, and having unloaded there the small craft still tie up beside Quay Road and the Barbican (to the old men this was 'The Quay'). Fishermen have to clamber over the rails, but they no longer land their catches on this side.

On the built-up side of the Barbican the postwar cafe built between Castle Street steps and the redbrick former railway parcel office is threatened with a rebuild as a Mayflower Information Centre. The ground floor of Island House now houses a city tourist information bureau, and behind in New Street the National Trust has a shop in the ground floor of the Elizabethan House. Further up New Street the Elizabethan Garden is now better laid out and maintained than it ever has been. Southside Street has a post office again, in the wine and food market.

PLYMOUTH GIN

Until 1996 the gin distillery at the top of Southside Street was owned by Whitbread, who also made Beefeater gin. Naturally enough their main gin interest was in Beefeater. So that when they hived off part of the building to become a Beefeater restaurant upstairs, with a lively bar on the ground floor, the only gin that they had on sale was Beefeater - in the distillery that made the rival Plymouth Gin. The atmosphere of a distillery has been admirably retained, and the vast copper stills first installed in 1855 and 1856 can be seen behind a glass screen.

These stills have never stopped making Plymouth Gin and three members of Whitbread's staff had such faith in the future of Plymouth Gin that, with three other friends, they were able to buy the whole distillery in 1996.

They still lease the restaurant and bar to the Beefeater restaurant division of Whitbread's. The new company, which has revived the name of Coates & Co, the original owners of Plymouth Gin, is making tremendous efforts to restore the fortune of Plymouth. The first step was to restore the strength of the home product to 40 per cent alcohol (which had, in keeping with most other gins, been reduced to 37 per cent), and to market an export gin at 57 per cent. The driving force and chairman of the new company is John Murphy, with Tom Absolom as managing director and Sean Harrison the distillery manager. They have kept the little shop in the front of the premises, and retained the summertime guided tours which are very popular.

BLACKFRIARS REPROGRAPHICS

Close to the distillery is the design, printing and photocopying firm called Blackfriars which employs a dozen people in Friars Lane and is the biggest single-unit reprographic plant in the South West. David King, who owns this plant with his son Simon, has been a major figure behind the changing Barbican scene. He started with a shop, which his wife ran, at the bottom of Southside Street selling specialist kitchen equipment and Dartington glass. He then bought a warehouse in White Lane which became the White Lane Gallery, and created craft workshops and six flats at the top. Another warehouse, on Vauxhall Quay, became Breton House with its three flats.

After a foray to Modbury, David's next Barbican project was to buy the old lemonade factory (behind the gin distillery) which had previously been the granary of Pitts & King, the maltsters. This was converted to a restaurant and gallery, two shops with two flats and an eight-bedroom hotel on the upper floors, all overlooking a courtyard. This was sold and became the Hosteria Romana. The business only survived for a few years before closing. In 1997 planning application was made to re-open the restaurant and convert the kitchens into craft workshops.

David and Simon King in 1970 started the reprographics in one of the buildings off the courtyard. As the machinery got bigger so various premises were used, including a tunnel below Palace Vaults and two buildings in Quay Road. The printing business ended up in what had been the meat factory of E. Dingle, the butcher, which had been built on the site of Holy Trinity Church. The existing catacombs were used for offset lino. The premises on Quay Road were converted into two shops and four flats.

ROBERT LENKIEWICZ

Opposite the gin distillery, at the top of Southside Street, is a former bonded warehouse whose back wall is at the top of the Parade. The ground floor, entered from Southside Street and labelled the Barbican Pannier Market, was occupied by fourteen stallholders selling collectibles, books, china, pictures, all sorts. All the upper floors had been occupied for years by Robert Lenkiewicz. In 1996

Robert Lenkiewicz, painter and philosopher, in a corner of his library.

a trust, the Lenkiewicz Foundation, was set up to take over the building and devote it to his work.

Robert was born in London of Jewish parents, refugees from Germany and before that Russia. Afer training at St Martin's School of Art and the Royal Academy schools, he settled in Plymouth in 1964, aged twenty-three. In those days the Barbican was the home of various itinerant artists, but Robert eventually finished up renting a shop, No 6 the Parade, from the Barbican Association. From this his pictures (he hardly ever sold a canvas and his output has been prodigious) and his enormous book collection, cover-

SUTTON HARBOUR

ing everything from fascism to magic but generally of a philosophical bent, has spread next door to all the top floors of the bonded warehouse.

Over the years he has produced a series of painting projects 'on humanist and sociological issues', ranging from vagrancy to orgasm and 'The Painter with Women'. They have always been controversial, and completely divorced from the work of most contemporary painters. He produced a vast mural on the walls of the warehouse, looking down on the Parade, and a smaller one on the other side, above Southside Street. In the 1990s he began to achieve national recognition, as well as local acceptance. His publicity stunts, such as advertising his death and disappearing for a few days, and his more explicit pictures, had outraged many people; but even they began to recognise his importance as a painter.

The trust aimed to convert the whole warehouse, as well as the Parade shop, into an art gallery and library devoted to his works, and to open both to scholars and the public. Grants were first promised by the Government's regeneration budget and were being sought from the European Regional Development Fund and the English Heritage Lottery Fund. The building would be converted internally to meet the objectives; on the outside, in place of the Parade mural, would be a huge stained glass window designed by Robert.

REVIVED CUSTOM HOUSE

The previous showpiece of the Parade was the Custom House, wonderfully restored and humming with activity. It was put up for sale in 1993 but the Government had second thoughts and instead spent millions on a refurbishment, inside and out. A particular joy is the old Long Room, restored as it was when built in 1820 with the double-vaulted ceiling picked out in two colours, elegant chandeliers and the Georgian fireplace at the end opened up again. It no longer serves its old purpose, where masters of arriving vessels would report, but is filled with desks.

The building became the control centre for the whole area west of a line from Bristol to Weymouth. It also houses Customs Investigation, Intelligence and anti-smuggling teams. They have offices in the old Queen's Warehouse behind the main building, and stretches through to Vauxhall Street. Here they have 'facilities for detention' (polite term for cells) as well as facilities for dealing with 'stuffers and swallowers', smugglers who secrete drugs inside their bodies.

What is more the Custom cutters are now berthed on a pontoon on the west side of Sutton Jetty, and it is quite common to see a couple of the big 120ft cutters alongside, with the smaller 70 footers tied up outside them. These are the craft that figure in the news reports, the grey shadows that watch smugglers all the way up from

Two Customs launches berthed alongside Sutton Jetty, close to the Custom House.

Gibraltar or intercept them in the chops of the Channel. Here they are berthed as near as they can be to the Custom House, and their coming and going all adds to the liveliness of the harbour.

SEA ANGLING

Plymouth sea anglers always claim that the port is the premier centre in this country for their sport. Between the Sutton Harbour office and Sutton Jetty are the pontoons of the sea angling club, from which a dozen or more fishing boats specially styled with big cockpits can be chartered. They take out the fishermen, who of a weekend will come from as far away as the Midlands to ply their sport on their chosen grounds - wrecks, the Eddystone rocks, Hand Deeps, wherever.

The Sea Angling club was started in 1969, when they took over Sutton Jetty, converting the warehouse there into a clubroom. By 1975 it had some two thousand members and fifteen boats attached. When the harbour company rebuilt the jetty, the late Jim Bryant, who had been running the club there, moved it to the present site on Little Vauxhall Quay and the club established pontoons in front.

After his death his son Phil took over; when he gave up the club it was re-opened in 1996 by Roy Powis, a businessman from Wolverhampton, in partnership with Geoff Lawlan. Mr Powis, who has since moved to Plymouth, had been fishing from the club several times each year for the previous twenty-seven years. Eventually Mr Lawlan took over what had become the rechristened Sea Angling and Water Sports Centre. The British Conger Club also has its headquarters in the club.

Over-fishing has reduced the size of catches of many species, and the number of charter boats has diminished accordingly. But the prestigous European Sea Angling championships have been held at the club in 1973, 1977, 1982, 1988 and 1994. This attracts up to two hundred competitors from all over Europe, from as far as Gibraltar and even South Africa. A number of local competitions are also held during the summer months, when the sport is most popular.

Boats berthed off the Sea Angling Club, next door to the Sutton Harbour Company's offices.

CINEMA, SNOOKER AND POP MUSIC

On the corner of Vauxhall Quay and Sutton Wharf, long occupied by Stidwell's wholesale fruit warehouse, is now the rather elegant entrance to the Quay snooker club, which is balanced at the other end of Sutton Wharf by the Plaza snooker club, upstairs in the former cinema. This opened in 1934, flourished as a 'second run' house and after the war became the place to see continental films. In its last days it had some renown for showing what were variously described as 'blue movies' and 'soft porn', and finally closed its doors in 1981. For some years after the the ground floor was an arcade of small shops but in 1985 it became an Indian restaurant.

Across Tin Lane the building where barrels had been made since 1800, the Cooperage, has become a night club which specialises in touring pop

SUTTON HARBOUR

groups. It flourished for many year as a a cooperage proper; when the demand for barrels began to collapse between the wars the owners, Lethbridge's, turned to making bookends and other souvenirs from the timbers of the old wooden battleship still being broken up in the Cattewater. After the war it had a long spell as a restaurant run by Peter Zeissimedes, who was one of the first Greek Cypriots to settle in the city after 1946.

NORTH QUAY TO MARROWBONE SLIP

From North Quay right round to the new fish market the harbour shoreline has changed almost out of recognition since 1980. Harbourside Court and Mariner's Court, with North Quay House opened in 1996, fill the whole of North Quay with just the empty site at the western end still awaiting development in 1997. When the two blocks of flats were completed they had between them two single-storey warehouses erected after the war and still working.

The Plymouth Co-operative Society's warehouse on North Quay, built in 1960, knocked down in 1990 to make way for a block of flats that in 1997 had still to be built.

Their last occupants were Plymouth Fruit Stores, which in 1994 moved out to Sutton Road. Sutton Harbour Development Company, who owned the North Quay site, then built a five-storey block of offices which they called North Quay House. The architects were Lacey, Hickie & Caley, whose base is just arround the corner in Salt Quay House. It is complementary in height to the blocks of flats on either side, and its pale buff facing-stone makes the transition from the limestone of Harbourside Court to the aggressive white of Mariner's Court, fortunately fading as time goes on. Opened in 1996, the top two floors were at once taken by English Partnership, which had worked very closely with the harbour company over the building and financing of the fish market.

The railway lines remain along the cobbled quay although the water's edge is part of the marina car park. The quay west of Hawker's Avenue, like the parking area on Sutton Quay, is marked off on the landward side with granite 'toadstools' which keep the maritime idea with their bollard-like appearance; east of Hawker's Avenue a line of the now standard harbour company's black iron posts define the parking area.

It is hard to realise that as late as 1936 quite large steamers and even three-masted sailing vesssels were still unloading at these quays.

The old warehouse backing North-East Quay, last used as a cement warehouse, was rebuilt by the harbour company in the early 1990s. The building has a slight curve, dictated by the railway lines behind; this was retained but the long roofline broken by a couple of gables. It is rented to marine-related firms.

On the far side of the Shipwright's Arms the harbour company cleared away the untidy and derelict old stone buildings which stretched right to Marrowbone Slip and rebuilt them with a modern structure which presented half a dozen prominent glass-fronted gables to the waterside. Among the tenants were yacht architects, a marine engine firm, and Harbour Marine. The local boat owners who had for centuries had free access to the sea on the uncluttered beaches of Marrowbone Slip were left with the slipway and part of their beach.

Old plans of the harbour show quays named after the cargoes handled across them, and the harbour company began using these quay names for their new buildings. The marina ablutions block with offices above on North Quay became Tin Quay House, the restored North-East Quay warehouse the Salt House, and the buildings housing Harbour Marine the Sugar Quay House. One old name not pressed into service is the Dung Quay!

PLYMOUTH FRUIT SALES

Sutton Road, the main artery of Coxside, had a newcomer to its normal run of builders' merchants, motor-related businesses, scrap metal merchants and the like, in 1995. Plymouth Fruit Sales had been started in a post-war warehouse in Hawkers Avenue ten years earlier. Two men each with thirty years experience in the wholesale trade, Ted Nancarrow and Dick Parsons, joined forces to start the company, six months before the first flat in Harbourside Court, opposite, was occupied

But they worked by night which was not compatible with the residential use of its neighbours; the harbour company who owned their warehouse wanted to develop the site, and so Plymouth Fruit moved, to Sutton Road. For two centuries at least fruit and vegetables had been a major concern of Sutton Harbour. When Plymouth Fruit opened their doors in 1985 there were thirteen wholesale fruiterers in the city; by 1997 there were only two. The dominance of the supermarkets, with their central purchasing, was killing the local traders. In spite of this the new company flourished, employing twenty people.

THE CHINA HOUSE

For years the China House, so named because reputedly Cookworthy stored his Plymouth porcelain there, stood empty. In 1992 Ansells Brewery leased it from Sutton Harbour and converted it into a pub and restaurant. Because of its age (built in 1650, it is the oldest water's edge warehouse surviving in Britain) the conversion was done very carefully; the only alteration to the outer appearance a central two storey gable and a promenade deck in front, and at the rear an extension to house kitchens and storerooms. The inside was given lofts, hoists, old fittings and ropes, with casks and crates about the place as if still in use. Information boards about the building give its general history; with special accounts of Cookworthy and of Shilston, the shipbuilder on the site. It was all very well done, and an instant success. With its car park and new quay wall at the head of Marrowbone Slip it completed the clean-up of the north-eastern side of the harbour right to Coxside Creek.

GOVERNMENT OFFICES

Behind the China House, on the west side of the creek, a four-storey office block was built to house government departments. This was a result of the decision to house all regional offices of the various ministries in one building, and to make Plymouth a joint regional centre with Bristol. Had it been on harbour company land it undoubtedly would have been called Shepherd's

SUTTON HARBOUR

Wharf House; as it is the name of Mast House has been adopted. This began to be occupied at the end of 1996, with a car park and gardens behind reaching back to Sutton Road.

HOTELS

On Sutton Road is the former warehouse of Rowe Brothers, fruit wholesalers, which had a brief life as a rival fish market. This is to be demolished to make way for an hotel which will front on the edge of Coxside Creek. Next door, on the former cement mixing works, is being built a forty-bedroom travel inn; ancillary rooms to the new pub, Lockyer's Quay Inn, which has been built on the infill site at the head of the creek. This recovered land, originally earmarked for an engineering and repair yard for the fishing fleet, was instead leased to Whitbread's the brewers who built this as a standard pub-cum-restaurant of a type found up and down the country, complete with a children's playground. It was opened at the end of 1996.

On the other side of Sutton Road, at the corner of Barbican Approach, a smart car showroom opened in 1996 by Bramall-Allen's, the local Vauxhall dealer, adds another note of sophistication. Its repair and service departments stretch back along Barbican Approach Road. The Thistle Park pub, on the opposite corner, in 1993 opened its own brewery, Sutton Brewery, alongside and is building a reputation as a real ale pub. For several years it has run a celebratory real ale festival.

THE NEW AQUARIUM

On the south side of the creek is the new multi-storey 'Barbican' car park. This will be better used when the National Marine Aquarium is completed behind it, on the edge of Dead Man's Bay.

This ambitious project, the brainchild of Dr Geoff Potts of the Marine Biological Association, is intended to replace the present aquarium on the ground floor of the MBA's laboratory on the Hoe. Instead of the old-fashioned large tanks there will be ten spectacular exhibits showing marine animals and plants in their natural habitat. The visit will start with a moorland stream, progress to the estuary, to an inshore sea area and on to the deep water, with all their various occupants. A tank showing a coral reef and its inhabitants will be seven metres high; another large tank will have a glass-lined tunnel through which visitors will walk with sharks and similar fish swimming all around and overhead.

This project, expected to attract half a million visitors a year, will have ample educational facilities, with an auditorium for lectures and an educational suite. The building will stretch along the shore line and at the western end, close to the new fish market, will be shops and refreshment facilities. Work started at the end of 1996 on building these ancillary wings, which will enclose a square open on the seaward side and looking across the mouth of the Plym to Mount Batten. The position of this refreshment area will in itself add immensely to the attractions of the area.

ALL CHANGE

When the Royal Western Yacht Club first opened its new clubhouse at Queen Anne's Battery, in 1989, there were members who complained of having to drive through dirty, rundown streets. That is all changing. While the entrance to Sutton Road from Exeter Street has its warehouses on both sides to proclaim its industrial history, they are spruced up and presentable.

On the seaward side, from the repainted Shipwright's Arms right out to the turning into the new car park and fish market, will be new buildings with glimpses past the China House to the harbour. The new hotel and travel lodge will bring a different and brighter view of life into the area, supported by the motor showrooms on the opposite corner. On the south side of Barbican Approach, bounded on the west by the nostalgically named Gashouse Lane, the site of the former gasworks has been bought by a development company who plan a multi-screen cinema and other entertainments.

The new pubs and offices, as well as the marina, the yacht club, and the fish market, all bring in people. The Aquarium will add to this popularity. The old industries of the pre-war years, like the gas works, the soap and candle works, the Eagle Steam Joinery (just the Eagle pub, and the eagle figures over the gates of a warehouse in Clare Place remain), have all disappeared. But the area has not forgotten its industrial origins, even if its products have changed. It is still the old mixture of trade and industry, residential and maritime.

In fact the whole of the area around Sutton Harbour is the fastest changing part of Plymouth. From the Barbican with its new life and its new buildings, around the North Quay area with its middle-class flat development, to Coxside with its fresh life and the transformed, blossoming fishing business, it is all change. The mixture is right; seafaring represented by the fishing and the yachts, industry still strong but replacing manufacture by services, housing representing the new improved standards of living; it is all shaping the right way. And of all the area, the long derelict Coxside streets and waterfront show the greatest changes.

If the QAB marina and the Royal Western Yacht Club started the regeneration of Coxside, then the enterprise and determination of the Sutton Harbour Company in building the lock gates, moving the fish market; reorganising its structure so that it could play a vigorous part in developing the shore areas around the harbour, has been the real catalyst.

Plymouth was born out of Sutton Harbour and the sea. Its future still depends on the use it makes of its maritime position, and its waterfront. And as the millennium approaches, so Sutton Harbour is still showing the rest of the city the way ahead.

Visiting reproduction historic ships exemplify the new Sutton Harbour, combining the best of the old with an eye to the future. Below, Captain Cook's ship Endeavour *in front of the Aquarium building, under construction, August 1997.*

INDEX

Admiralty 13-14, 18, 25, 28, 34, 37, 45, 57, 94
Admiralty House 28
Alma Street 68
Alsop, William 88
Amadas, Philip 58
America 15, 23, 30, 41, 43, 58, 60, 62, 65, 81, 83-84
Amethyst, HMS 86-87
Andrews, Graham 100
Anglicans 74, 76, 79, 104
Ansells Brewery 115
Antonucci, Michael 103
Appledore 63
Argyle, Duke of 15
Armada, The Spanish 23, 51, 58, 74, 108
Armada Gallery 108
Armada Way 74
Artisans Dwellings Company 78
Arts Centre 73, 83
Arundell, Lord 12, 50
Astor, Lady 22
Australia 17, 61-65

Baltic Wharfs 62, 92
Banks, Joseph 85
Banks, Josiah 83
Barber, James 49, 68, 106
Barbican 15, 19, 21-23, 25-26, 31-32, 38, 43, 47, 49-50, 53, 55-57, 60, 69-71, 74-75, 77, 79-80, 91-95, 103-111, 116-117
Barbican Angling Marina 57
Barbican Approach 116-117
Barbican Association 77, 79, 93, 103, 111
Barnes, Francis 8, 74
Bates, Sir Edward 78, 91
Batten Breakwater 57
Batten, Captain 24
Batter Street 68, 77, 103-104
Bayly, Richard 14
Bayly, Robert 19, 56, 69
Baylys of Island House 84
Beaumont House 12
Bedford, John 77
Bedford Place 42
Bellamy, Sir Joseph 19, 80
Bethel 74-75, 104
Bideford 46, 101
Blachford, Lord 42, 62
Black Ball 64

Black Friars 81
Black Prince, The 11, 21, 85
Blackfriar Print 74
Blackfriars Lane 82
Blake, Admiral 93, 101
Blake, Robert 24
Bligh, Captain William 61
Blitz (Plymouth) 72, 76, 82, 90
Board of Health 70
Board of Improvement Commissioners 77
Board of Ordnance 25
Bonaparte, Napoleon 72
Bond, J.T. 78
Bordeaux 21, 39
Boringdon, Lord 14, 67
Boston 61
Both St 73-74
Bottle Hill 52
Bounty, HMS 61
Bovisand 92
Bowling Green 42
Brahaut, Captain 69
Bramall-Allen 116
Breakwater, The 47, 49, 52, 57, 90
Breton Boys 66
Breton House 111
Bretonside 7, 14, 21, 47, 66-67, 72, 76, 81-82, 90, 103-104, 106
Brewhouse 110
Bridge Road 84
Bristol 15, 18, 29, 41-42, 83, 86, 112, 115
Britayne Side 66
British Conger Club 113
Brittany 40
Brixham 25, 29-31, 37-38, 86, 93, 101
Brock, Cissie 103
Brock House 68, 77, 103, 106
Brock Trust, The 103
Bromley, Peter 8, 100
Brunel, I.K. 15-17, 52, 88, 94
Brunswick Terrace 68-69
Bryant & May 90-91, 113
Bryant, Jim 113
Buckingham Gate 12
Buckland Abbey 15, 77
Buckwell Street 66, 73, 78
Bunch of Grapes 71
Burnard, Robert 90-91
Burnell, John 90
Burton Boys (*see* Breton Boys)

Cabot, John 29
Canada 62-63
Candish, Thomas 23
Cape Cod 59
Cape of Good Hope 40, 62, 64
Cap'n Jasper's cafe 109-110
Carne, James 73
Castle Dyke 71, 78
Castle Dyke Lane 71, 78
Castle Rag 71
Castle Street 70-72, 74-75, 78-79, 81, 95, 104, 110
Catherine Street 42, 61, 66, 77, 104
Cattedown 15, 47-48, 55-56, 66, 84, 91, 93
Cattedown Corner 68
Cattedown Road 55, 104
Cattedown Wharf 93
Cattewater 9, 14-15, 21, 23-25, 28, 31, 42-46, 56-57, 64, 75, 91, 114
Cawsand 29, 43, 107, 109
Cawsey 49
Central Hall 67, 90
Champion, Richard 83
Chant, John 36
Charles I, King 59
Charles II, King 12, 24
Charlestown 67, 69
Chatham 25
Chichester, Sir Francis 23, 72
China House 24-25, 28, 54, 83-87, 106, 115, 117
China House Yard 86
Cholera 64, 70, 73
Citadel Ope 38, 108
Citadel Road 74, 105
Civic Trust 105
Civil War 12, 24, 30, 61, 66
Clare Buildings 78
Clare House 84, 90-91
Clare Mission 76
Clare Place 76, 117
Clare Street 84
Clarence, Duke of 22, 72
Clarke, Irving 17
Clements, Dorothy 107
Cload, C. R. 108
Cochrane, Lord 27, 42, 82
Cock, Captain Lucas 51
Cock, Lucretia 51
Cook, Captain James 61, 83
Co-operative Society 19, 114

Colonial Land Funds 64
Commercial Wharf 26, 32, 63, 91
Compton, Roger 108
Condy, Nicholas 51
Cookworthy, William 14, 69, 83-84, 88, 115
Copenhagen, Battle of 61
Cornwall 8, 11-12, 18, 29, 62-63, 70, 77, 83, 91
Courtenay, Peter 12
Coxside 9, 18, 25, 38, 46-47, 51-55, 57, 68, 76, 78, 83-85, 87-92, 94-95, 97-98, 115-117
Coxside Corner 68
Coxside Creek 47, 52, 84, 91, 94-95, 97-98, 115-116
Coxside Gas Works 88
Coxside Station 55
Crane Quay 49
Crocker, H. 43
Cromwell, Oliver 25
Crownhill 90
Custom House 8, 43-44, 50, 86, 112-113
Custom House Quay 43, 86

Dalton, Percy 85
Dame Hannah Rogers School 42
Damnation Alley 71, 74
Dartington 109, 111
Dartmoor 13, 18-19, 23, 39, 48, 52-53, 55, 91
Dartmoor Prison 13
Dartmouth 29-30, 39, 41, 58, 60
Devon Railway Company 16
Devonport 9, 17, 41, 43, 85, 103, 105
Dogfish 33-35
Dolphin Court 46, 57, 88, 103
Dolphin House 45, 55
Donovan, Sonia 108
Dover 41, 101
Down, Rex 100
Drake, Sir Francis 23-24, 29, 40, 58, 69, 77
Drake Circus 84
Drake's Island 99
Duchy of Cornwall 8, 12
Dudley, John 109
Dung Quay 50, 52, 106, 115
Dunstan, Lovell 34, 108

Eagle Steam Joinery 117
East India Company 41
East Pier 94-95
Ebrington Street 74, 76
Eddystone 29, 47, 113
Edward I, King 11, 21, 29
Edward IV, King 22
Edward Island 63, 86, 88
Edwards, Peter 8
Efford Manor 17
Elaine W. 93
Eldad 16-17
Elford, Henry 91
Elford, William 13-14, 52
Eliot, John 40
Elizabeth I, Queen 23, 40, 58
Elizabethan Garden 77, 110
Elizabethan House 42, 79, 110
Elphinstone 64-65
Elphinstone Wharf 62
Embankment 67, 88
Embankment Road Methodist Church 88
Emden, Martin 8, 99
Emigration 62-65, 74, 91
Endeavour, The 61
English Partnerships 104
Exeter 12, 15-18, 30, 41, 53, 55, 66-70, 74-76, 80, 106, 116
Exeter Railway 18
Exeter Road 66
Exeter Street 12, 53, 55, 68-70, 74-76, 80, 116

Falmouth Steam Packet Company 43
Farr, Grahame 86
First World War 19, 43-44, 46, 92
Fish and fishing 8, 9, 11, 19, 21, 24, 29-35, 37-39, 44, 46, 48-50, 56-57, 81, 83-94, 98-101, 103-107, 109-110, 114, 116-117
Fish House 24, 48-49
Fish Quay 57, 110
Foot, Isaac 34, 69, 76, 80, 83, 88
Foster, Brian 99
Fowell, John 12
Fowey 39
Fox-Smith, William 82, 104, 108
Frean, George 91
Free Church Missions 74

118

INDEX

Freedom Fields 66
Friars Lane 110
Friary Court 73
Friary Gardens 53
Friary Green 69
Friary Quay 51
Friary Station 54
Friary Street 51, 85
Furneaux, Tobias 61

Galbraith, W.R. 53
Gashouse Lane 117
Gate Secondary Modern School 79
Gaveston, Piers 11
George II, King 12
George III, King 26, 67
George Street 66, 75, 84
George Tavern 27
Gibbons, Stanley 80
Gilbert, Ralegh 59
Gill, Thomas 15-16, 62, 91
Gin 66, 81, 82, 110
Glue-making 84
Godefroy, Duncan 7-8, 20, 98, 100
Gordon, Admiral 93, 101
Gorges, Sir Ferdinando 58
Grand Banks 30
Gray, Robert 13
Great House 66, 69
Great Tree 51
Great Western Railway 15-16, 18, 31, 32, 52, 53-56, 86
Greenbank 77, 85
Greenbank Terrace 85
Greenhill, Basil 86
Greenwich 8
Guernsey Packet 73
Guildhall 13-15, 22, 61, 66
Guildhall Square 34

Hall, Humphrey 12, 14
Hamoaze 9, 25, 27
Hand Deeps 113
Hannam, Elizabeth 107
Hanover House 103
Harbour Avenue 55, 75, 103
Harbour Marine 102, 115
Harbourside Court 82, 103, 114-115
Harris, Andrew Saunders 19
Harris, Bill Best 8
Harrison, Sean 110
Hatchard, John 71, 73
Hawke, Admiral 26
Hawker, Colonel John 13-14, 82

Hawker, Robert (of Morwenstow) 73
Hawkers Avenue 81-82, 115
Hawkins, John 23, 40, 76
Hawkins, William 40, 50
Henry VII, King 40
Henry VIII, King 23, 49, 69
Hewer, Robert 12
High Street 49, 66, 73, 83
Hill Quarry 95
Hill Road 88
Hill Street 78
Hobart Street 15
Hodges, William
Hoe 11, 15, 23, 25, 43, 47, 60, 63, 66-67, 69, 78, 102, 105, 107, 116
Hoe Approach 105
Hoegate Street 17, 67, 69, 76-77, 83, 107
Holy Trinity Church 73-74, 79, 88, 111
Holy Trinity Schools 74
Honicknowle 80
Hooe Lake 49
Hospital of Poor 61
Howe Street 52, 104
Hudson Bay Company 65
Hudson River 59
Huguenots 98
Hull 37, 41, 90
Hundred Years War 21

Improvement Company Act 53
Inglis, J. C. 56
Interfish 93, 101
Ireland 15, 41, 44, 58, 64, 70
Island House 61, 69, 84, 110
Isles of Scilly 33

Jacka, Frederick 108
Jacka, Hugh 108
Jago, Tony 109
James I, King 58
Jamestown 58-59
Jennycliffe 92
Jersey 73, 92, 101
Jervis, Admiral Sir John 83
Jews 42
John, King of France 21
Jolly Young Waterman 71
Jones, Christopher 59

Kennebec 58
King Street 17, 65, 70, 79
Kingsbridge 83, 91, 110
Kingsley, Sir Patrick 8
Kinsman, Andrew 76

Kinterbury Street 69, 76
Kitto, John 79-80
Knight, Christopher 109

Laing, David 43
Laira 9, 17-18, 48, 52-53, 57, 67, 85, 105
Laira Bridge 48, 52, 57, 105
Lambhay 21, 25-26, 47, 61-62, 71-72, 74, 78, 91, 109
Lambhay Hill 21, 71, 74, 109
Lambhay Street 72, 78
Lambhay Victualling Yard 62
Lane, Ralph 58
Lane, Thomas 14
Langmead, Philip 13
Lawlan, Geoff 113
Lawrence (of Arabia) 28
Lenkiewicz, Robert 79, 108-109, 111
Lethbridge (family) 87, 88, 114
Lipson Road 67
Little Vauxhall Quay 51-53, 113
Lock gates 9, 16, 18, 94-95, 97-98, 106, 109, 117
Locke, Joseph 53
Lockyer, Edmund 52
Lockyer Quay 38, 48, 52, 57, 94-95, 98, 107, 116
London 14-15, 17-18, 30, 39, 41-42, 44, 46, 53, 58-59, 62, 80, 86, 90-91, 111
London Company of Virginia 59
Longford, H, J. 19
Looe Street 50, 52, 69-70, 72-73, 78, 83, 104
Lower Lane Mission 76
Lower Street 69, 75, 104
Lowestoft 31, 35-36
Luscombe, William 19, 56, 94
Lyth, Shaun 8, 100

McBride, Admiral John 12-13, 21, 71
McCauley, Dan 99
Mackerel 30, 35, 38, 93-94, 101
Macrath, Sir George 17
Madiera Road 63
Manadon 12
Maritime Inn 72
Maritime Trust 46
Marrowbone Slip 25, 72, 84, 86-87, 102, 114-115
Marryat, Captain 82
Marshall, Pat 99
Marshall, William 30

Marsh Mills 53
Martin Lane 66
Marychurch 29
Mast House 116
Maton, W. G. 30
May, Francis 90
Mayflower 23, 26, 49, 59-61, 65, 72, 92, 105, 107, 109
Mayflower Pier 105, 107, 109-110
Mayflower Sailing Club 26, 92
Mayflower Steps 107
Mayflower Stone 49, 65
Mayoralty House 68, 77, 104
Meeting House Slip 85, 90
Methodism 74, 76, 83, 88, 90
Methodist Central Hall 90
Mill Lane 88, 90-91
Millbay 13, 15-18, 31-32, 44-46, 52, 54, 56, 87, 90-91, 94
Millbay Pier 15-16
Millbay Road 17
Millbay Soap Works 91
Millbrook 26, 39, 107
Millbrook Steam Company 107
Mimosa 45
Minerva 72
Ministry of Agriculture 38, 98
Ministry of Defence 20, 105
Modbury 111
Modley, J.W. 19, 37
Moon Street 70, 74, 78
Moore, Joseph 85
Morley, Earl of 14, 17, 63
Mount Batten 24, 27-28, 33-34, 105, 116
Mount Wise 27-28, 47, 105
Murphy, John 110
Mutley 33
Mutton Cove 85
Mutual Steam Fishing Co. 37
My Lady 86
Nabisco 91
Nancarrow, Ted 115
Napoleon Inn 73
Napoleonic Wars 26, 42, 84-85
Nash, Jack 108
Nash, James L. 88, 108
National Marine Aquarium 98, 107, 116
National Trust 110
Naval Air Station 34
Naval Reserve Inn 73
Navy Inn 50, 72
Nelson, Admiral Lord 17, 26, 61, 71, 91
New George Street 66, 84

New Patent Candle Company 90
New Street 35, 42, 61, 66-67, 70-71, 77-79, 100, 103-104, 108, 110
New Zealand Company 61-62
Newfoundland 29-30, 44, 46, 59, 86-87
Newlyn 35, 37-38, 93, 101
Newman, Michael 76
Nicholls, W. 37
Nonsuch 65
North-East Quay 54-55, 57, 85, 102, 114-115
North Friary House 85
North Hill 42, 47
North Quay 19, 45-46, 53, 55, 57, 66, 69, 76, 81, 102-103, 106, 110, 114-115, 117
North Quay House 69, 106, 114
North Street 51, 67, 76
Notte Street 47, 66, 69, 73-74, 76-78, 80-81, 83, 88, 105

Ocean Quay 54
Odgers, W. J. 70
Old Custom House 50
Old Plymouth Society 79
Old Ring of Bells 72
Old Tabernacle 76
Old Town Boys 66
Old Town Without 67
Old Tree Slip 53, 67, 69, 72, 81
Opie, S. A. 8
Ordnance Board 62
Ord, Ralph 72
Oreston 84, 91

Parade, The 27, 32, 41, 43-44, 49-50, 53, 56, 66, 68, 72, 74, 79-80, 88, 94, 104, 106, 108-109, 111-112
Parsons, Ray 100
Pearn, William 53
Pepys, Samuel 25
Pitts, Thomas 19, 56
Plymouth Great Western Dock Company 18
Plymouth Sound 39, 47, 72, 107
Plymouth Trawler Agents 8, 100
Plymouth Trawlers Ltd 36-37
Plymouth Venturer 107
Plympton 11, 52, 90
Plymstock 90
Pocohontas 59

119

SUTTON HARBOUR

SuttonPool 7, 11-15, 17-18, 20-26, 30, 34, 38-39, 41-42, 44-51, 54, 57-59, 61, 65-66, 85, 91-92
Poor Clares 84
Pope, John 18
Portsmouth 25, 39, 43, 100
Portugal 21, 30, 39, 41, 82
Portwrinkle 29
Potts, Dr Geoff 116
Powis, Roy 113
Press Gangs 26-27
Pridham 14
Prince Edward Island 63, 86, 88
Prince Rock 78, 106
Princess Square 34
Princetown 13, 25, 52
Prysten House 50
Public Health Act 77
Puritans 12, 59, 60-61
Puseyites 74
Pye, Andrew 8

Quakers 83, 90
Quarrying 15, 52, 90, 95
Quay House 69, 106, 114-115
Quay Inn 116
Quay Road 56, 103, 105, 107, 109-111, 117

Railways 5, 7, 15-18, 20, 30-32, 38, 44-45, 47, 49, 51-57, 62, 109-110, 114
Raleigh, Sir Walter 58
Ray, Dr Keith 8, 106
Reading, Lord 34
Regent Street 67
Rendell, J.M. 52
Resolution 61
Richard II, King 21, 39
Rising Sun 71
Roanoke Island 58
Robin Hood 71, 103
Robin Starch 90
Roebuck 58
Rogers, Frederic 62
Rolfe, John 59
Roman Catholics 23, 76
Roscoff 46
Rossfish 100
Rotolox 99
Rowe Brothers 100, 116
Royal Air Force 28
Royal Academy 111
Royal Albert Hospital 103
Royal Army Service Corps 28
Royal Artillery 28
Royal Australian Air Force 28
Royal Citadel 24

Royal Dockyard 20
Royal Marines 15, 27-28
Royal Naval Engineering College 12
Royal Naval Hospital 25, 83
Royal Regiment of Invalids 28
Royal Veteran Battalion 28
Royal Western Yacht Club 15, 116-117
Royal William Yard 26, 62, 91, 105

St James of Compostello 39
St John-Sutton-on-Plym 104
St Germans, Earls of 40
Salcombe 39, 86
Salt House 72, 81, 115
Salt Quay House 114
Saltash 11, 38-39
Saltram 14, 26
Salvation Army Hall 76
Sanders Stevens 37, 80
Sawyers Arms 72
Scallops 38, 93
Scott, Robert Falcon 17, 83
Sea Angling Club 57, 113
Sea Hawke 37
Second World War 19, 28, 44, 55, 76, 82, 86, 92, 103, 108
Serpell, Robert 91
Seven Years War 41
Sewage treatment 106
Seymour Road 14
Shaftesbury Cottages 78
Shell Co. 37-38
Shepherd, William 84
Sherwell 76, 91
Shilston 28, 85-86, 115
Ship Inn 50, 72
Shipbreaking 86
Shipbuilding 39, 63, 85-86
Shipwrights 72-73, 85, 102, 114, 116
Simple, Peter 82
Sirius 15
Simpson, William 13, 49
Slums 70, 75, 78, 85
Smallpox 77
Smarte, John 50
Smith, Captain John 59, 60
South Africa 113
South Devon Railway 16, 18
South Devon Shipping Company 43, 86, 90
South Devon Terrace 68
South West Water 106

South Western Gas Board 90
South-Western Railway Company 18, 53
Seymour, Sir Michael 14
Somers, Sir George 59
Southampton 17-18, 41, 56, 60
Southern Belle 107
Southside Ope 27
Southside Street 9, 27, 34, 47, 51, 56, 66-67, 69, 71-73, 80-82, 88, 93, 103-105, 107-112
Sparke, John 12, 103
Speedwell 60
Spooners 77
Standish, Miles 60
Stannaries 13
Steamboat Company 91
Stedman, Peter 8, 20, 99
Stert, Arthur 25
Stevens, John 80
Stevens, Marshall 80
Stevens, Robert 80
Stillman Street 79
Stonehouse 9, 17, 19, 25-27, 39, 54, 56, 62, 83, 88, 91
Stonehouse Gas Co. 88
Stonehouse Herald 17
Stonehouse Lane 17
Stonehouse Pool 54
Sugar House 102
Sugar Quay House 115
Sun Brewery 83
Sutton Brewery 116
Sutton Harbour Company 4, 7, 20, 33, 38, 43, 51, 72-73, 95, 100, 102, 113, 117
Sutton Harbour Development Company 114
Sutton Harbour Fisheries Ltd 99
Sutton Harbour Holdings 99
Sutton Harbour Improvement Company 7-9, 18-19, 32, 53, 80, 99, 103
Sutton Harbour Railway Station 53
Sutton Harbour Services Ltd 99, 102
Sutton Jetty 28, 56-57, 102, 112-113
Sutton Pool 7, 11-15, 17-18, 20-26, 30, 34, 39, 41-42, 44, 46-48, 50-51, 58-59, 61, 65-66, 85, 91-92
Sutton Pool Act 14
Sutton Prior 12-13
Sutton Quay 45-46, 57, 103, 114

Sutton Road 12, 47, 53, 55, 66, 76, 79, 84, 90-91, 102, 104, 114-116
Sutton Valletort 12
Sutton Wharf 48-49, 51-53, 55-57, 73, 87-88, 102, 113
Sutton-on-Plym 74
Sutton-super Plymouth 106
Swan Vestas 90
Swift 92
Swilly 61, 78

Tamar Cruising 107
Tamar Housing Society 103
Tamaritans 75
Tavistock 18, 39-40
Teate, Thomas 49
Thistle Park Tavern 88
Thompson, Amyas 60
Thompson, David 60
Thompson, Zoe 8
Three Crowns 44, 72
Three Towns 72
Tin Lane 52, 113
Tin Quay 52, 115
Tin Quay House 115
Tin Street 52
Tolls 14, 32, 43
Tolpuddle Martyrs 72
Tope, R. B. 88
Tor Royal 13
Torbay Fish Ltd 38
Torres Vedras 82
Town Gate 67
Tregenna, Edward 12
Trematon 11
Treville Street 43, 79-80, 104
Trinity Church 73, 111
Turner, Charles W. 19
Turner, Percy 36-37
Turnchapel 14, 42, 48, 56, 63, 88, 91
Tyrwhitt, Thomas 13, 52

Union Street 17-18, 76, 104
United Services 42

Vauxhall Quay 49-53, 55, 94, 103, 111, 113
Vauxhall Street 27, 43, 47, 49, 52, 69, 72, 104, 106, 112
Veale, Thomas 12
Vennel Street 73
Victoria Soap Company 91
Victoria, Queen 78
Victoria Wharf 57
Victualling Office 25-26, 63, 91
Victually Yard 84

Vinegar Hill 67
Vintry Ward 108
Virginia 41, 59, 83 W.

Wakefield, Edward Gibbon 61
Water Sports Centre 113
Water Transport Company 28
Weir Head 107
Welcome Home Sailor 71
Werninck, J.G. 42
Wesley, John 75-76
Wesleyans 75
West Indies 43, 61, 81
West of England Soap Company 90-91
West Pier 11, 31, 47, 48, 54, 56, 59, 61, 65, 80, 91, 95, 97, 109
Western Belle 107
Western Daily Mercury 78
Western Lass 86
Western Morning News 8
Weston Maid 107
Weymouth 58, 112
Wharf House 116
Whimple Street 66
White House Pier 56, 109
White Lane Gallery 111
Whitefriars 21
Whitfeld, Henry 78
William IV, King 72, 85
William of Orange 25
William Yard 62, 91, 105
Williams, Stephen 107
Willow, Irene 102
Willow, Michael 102
Windsor Lane 74
Wine 13-14, 21, 26, 29, 39-44, 81-82, 103-104, 107, 110
Woodrow, C.J. 19
Woodrow, Jim 103
Woollcombe, Henry 14, 17-18, 62
Woollcombe, Thomas 18, 62
Woolster Street 47, 72-73, 77
Woolwich 25
Woolworths 84
Worth, Hansford 19
Worth, R.N. 8, 65

Yarmouth Stores 108
Yealm 39, 107
Yealmpton 47, 88
Yogge (family) 22, 40, 69
Yonge, 17

Zeebrugge 101
Zeissimedes, Peter 114